WE

ARE SMARTER THAN

ME

HOW TO UNLEASH THE POWER OF
CROWDS IN YOUR BUSINESS

WE
ARE SMARTER THAN
ME

HOW TO UNLEASH THE POWER OF
CROWDS IN YOUR BUSINESS

BARRY LIBERT & JON SPECTOR
AND THOUSANDS OF CONTRIBUTORS

Vice President, Publisher: Tim Moore
Associate Editor-in-Chief and Director of Marketing: Amy Neidlinger
Editor: Yoram (Jerry) Wind
Editorial Assistant: Pamela Boland
Development Editor: Russ Hall
Digital Marketing Manager: Julie Phifer
Publicist: Amy Fandrei
Marketing Coordinator: Megan Colvin
Cover Designer: Ingredient
Managing Editor: Gina Kanouse
Senior Project Editor: Kristy Hart
Copy Editor: Krista Hansing Editorial Services, Inc.
Proofreader: Williams Woods Publishing
Senior Indexer: Cheryl Lenser
Interior Designer: Ingredient
Compositor: Jake McFarland
Manufacturing Buyer: Dan Uhrig

ISBN-10 0-13-216813-8
ISBN-13 978-0-13-216813-7

Pearson Education LTD.
Pearson Education Australia PTY, Limited.
Pearson Education Singapore, Pte. Ltd.
Pearson Education North Asia, Ltd.
Pearson Education Canada, Ltd.
Pearson Educatión de Mexico, S.A. de C.V.
Pearson Education—Japan
Pearson Education Malaysia, Pte. Ltd.

Library of Congress Cataloging-in-Publication Data is on file.

Cover images © 2007 Reimar Gaertner and World of Stock; Jan Tove Johansson/
Taxi/Getty Images; Gandee Vasan/Image Bank/Getty Images

This product is printed digitally on demand. This book is the paperback version
of an original hardcover book.

Contents

Foreword—Social Networking Works
by Don Tapscott

Many people emphasize the *social* aspect of social networking.
MySpace is growing at 2 million new registrants per week and with
over 200 million members, is well on its way to half a billion. Most
college students in the United States are on Facebook. There is a
new blog created every second of every day. Over a million avatars
live in a virtual community called Second Life.

But the smartest leaders see that the profitable word to emphasize
when it comes to social networking is *working*. Deep down, nothing
less than a new mode of production is in the making.

After all, if you can make an encyclopedia (Wikipedia) via social
networking and mass collaboration, what else could you do?
How about an operating system (Linux) or applications software
(Sugar CRM is one of 125,000 open source applications projects
underway)? How about a mutual fund (marketocracy.com), a peer-
to-peer lending system (zopa.com), or designer T-shirts (threadless.
com)? How about producing a television ad for the Super
Bowl? Viewers of this year's Super Bowl XLI watched a Doritos
advertisement that was created and chosen by its customers on the
Internet. Perhaps a complex physical good like a motorcycle? The
Chinese motorcycle industry—now the largest in the world—is
a sprawling network of parts makers with no single company like
Harley Davidson pulling the strings. Or take one of the world's the
most complicated products—a new generation jumbo jet. Rather
than painstakingly designing its supply chain, Boeing coinnovated
the 787 Dreamliner with thousands of partners around the world
in a mind-boggling peer-oriented ecosystem.

In this new world of collaboration, peers often come together to create value, often outside the walls of traditional companies. Consumer goods giant Procter & Gamble is a perfect example. Until recently, P&G was notoriously secretive, and it was failing, punctuated by a stock collapse in 2000. New CEO A. G. Lafley led the company on an ambitious campaign to restore P&G's greatness by sourcing 50 percent of its innovations from outside the company. Today, P&G searches for innovations in Web-enabled marketplaces such as InnoCentive, NineSigma, and yet2.com. These so-called eBays for innovation have led to hundreds of new products, some of which turned out to be home runs. Five years after the stock implosion, P&G has doubled its share price and now boasts a portfolio of 22 billion-dollar brands.

Around the same time, gold-mining company Goldcorp was in a similar pickle. Its geologists could not determine whether its ailing mines held any more ore. The corporation was on the brink of folding. CEO Rob McEwan did something unheard of in his industry. He published all of the company's previously secret geological data on the Web and held a contest to so see if anyone could help find gold on the property. Seventy-seven submissions came from around the world, some using techniques and technologies Goldcorp had not heard of. For $500,000 in prizes, Goldcorp found over $3 billion of gold and the company's market value multiplied several times over. By opening up and collaborating, Goldcorp's shareholders prospered.

Predictably however, revolutionary new modes of production bring dislocation and confusion. They are often received with coolness or worse—outright mockery or hostility. Vested interests fight against change. Leaders of the old have great difficulty embracing the new. Others are concerned that the incentives for knowledge producers are disappearing in a world where individuals can pool their talents to create free goods that compete with proprietary marketplace offerings. People as wise as Bill Gates have argued that capitalism is undermined by any movement to assemble a global "creative commons" that contains large bodies of scientific and cultural content. They fear that these massive communities and new business models will reduce the proportion of our economy available for profitable activity.

The examples in this book suggest otherwise. With more than a billion individuals around the world connected by a new multimedia high-bandwidth medium of human communications, collaboration and teamwork have become the business world's biggest drivers of success. Companies are eclipsing competitors by linking with suppliers and customers to share information, innovate, and execute. By harnessing the wisdom and ability of individuals and crowds, both inside and outside their boundaries, smart companies in every industry are thriving.

This is likely the first book you have read, created in collaboration with a crowd, and as such, I hope you will remember it and find it useful. But it won't be your last. My hope is that it may inspire you to get involved in the mass collaboration revolution and, in doing so, engage with others, have fun, and prosper.

> **Don Tapscott,** Chief Executive of the think tank
> New Paradigm and the author of 11 books, most
> recently, with Anthony D. Williams, *Wikinomics:*
> *How Mass Collaboration Changes Everything*

Authors' Note—How We Got Here

Five years ago, when we first had the experience that led to this book, the notion that a group might be smarter than any of its members was a complete non-starter. By definition, groupthink was the lowest common denominator; everyone knew that a camel was a horse designed by a committee. Today, thanks to a clutch of best-selling books, we know better. But even now, although crowdsourcing, wikinomics, and open-source technology have become buzzwords in the business world, there is no practical guide to translate those concepts into usable tools and techniques. This book fills that gap, describing in detail how businesses of all kinds can make the wisdom of crowds work for them. It's intended for all those businesspeople who want to tap into the power and talent of the online masses and are wondering how to go about it.

We stumbled on the basic idea as colleagues in a rapidly growing startup. One of the companies we acquired specialized in call-center management. The company had assembled a group of 200 executives, each of them running one or more call centers. These people actively collaborated with each other and collectively knew more about call centers than just about anyone. So when one of them was faced with a technical or strategic problem, he or she could turn to the other members of the group for advice, and count on getting it. In effect, rather than functioning simply as individual managers who turned to consultants for assistance, the members had learned to work as a community, and consistently offered each other collective advice that no single person or consultant could possibly provide.

For Barry, that story triggered the insight that led to this book. His idea was that companies of every kind could profitably and cost-effectively make the most of the knowledge and resources held by communities of like-minded people, whether they were employees, customers, partners, or investors. He went on to expand the call-center business into a company dedicated to helping other organizations tap the power of community. He called it Shared Insights.

Barry decided that a book was needed to share his rapidly growing experience and knowledge with a wider audience. But true to the basic concept, he didn't want to write it himself. It should be produced by a community, whose collectively shared ideas and insights would inevitably be better than any single author's.

Meanwhile, Jon was embarking on a new career as an educator. In 2004, he was named vice dean and director of executive education at The Wharton School of the University of Pennsylvania. A few months later, he learned Barry was looking for a partner to build the community that would write this book. Soon Jon signed onto the project.

The timing was serendipitous. James Surowiecki's *The Wisdom of Crowds*, which suggested that the masses have an intelligence that exceeds that of traditional experts, was a best seller. An even more widely read book, *Wikinomics: How Mass Collaboration Changes Everything*, by Don Tapscott and Anthony D. Williams, was to follow, showing how some companies are using mass collaboration and open-source technology to beat the competition. Wikipedia, the online encyclopedia whose content is produced by its readers, had become an Internet staple. Thomas Friedman's *The World Is Flat* would suggest that not only are crowds smart, they are highly connected and can do wondrous things. The irony was that hardly anyone except Wikipedia was actually mobilizing collective writing—as Surowiecki himself noted dryly, "I alone wrote this book." Our book would be the first of its kind, a breakthrough project. And Jon knew just the right publisher for a book written by a community.

The year before, Wharton had reached an agreement with Pearson Education to create and distribute business books. The two organizations were intrigued by Barry's proposal, and thus we began to hammer out an agreement with Wharton and Pearson as our publishers and supporters of the proposed book-writing community.

That's when some hard questions surfaced. With a community of hundreds or potentially thousands of people taking part in the writing, who would get what share of the royalties? Who would own the intellectual property? How would decisions be made about which chapters to include and what text to select?

We finally set up www.wearesmarter.org in the fall of 2006. It explained our goal, and nearly 3,000 people responded almost immediately. They had all sorts of ideas about how communities could help businesses and how the book could be put together. They also requested, appropriately, that we support the new community with a full cadre of moderators. Our project was, for a time, overwhelmed

as bloggers, podcasters, potential authors, and would-be
editors joined the community. Many also attended the first
Community 2.0 event in Las Vegas. In the end, we found
the actual text of the book, the flow of the topics, and the
graphical design had to be produced in the conventional
way, rather than relying on the crowd to perform these
functions. But it is fair to say that what you are reading is
a combination of our community's insights from all these
activities and our own research. And the callout quotes you
will find scattered throughout the book are drawn directly
from our members' wikis, podcasts, discussion posts, and
in-person comments from the Community 2.0 event.

The hard questions got solved. The community agreed that
the royalties would go to charity, and every person who
contributed to the project will have an equal voice in selecting
which charities will get the money.

Furthermore, the online community is still very much alive.
As of spring 2007, there were 4,375 members, 737 discussion
forum posts, and more than 250 wiki contributors generating
1,600 wiki posts. And we are planning another book in which
even more of the community's case studies and contributions
will be included.

In hindsight, the story of our community-driven odyssey
is an exciting tale, with ups and downs that are not all that
uncommon when ground-breaking initiatives are attempted.
As we point out in the pages ahead, many companies have
benefited hugely from harnessing collective power. But not all
have succeeded. As we will also detail, there are many pitfalls
to be avoided and obstacles to be overcome in tapping the
wisdom of communities.

If you are willing to take on the challenge, you have a good
chance of being handsomely rewarded. Communities can
help companies—your company—invent new products
and services, improve customer service, boost sales, turbo-
charge manufacturing, tap into new sources of financing, and
make everyone a leader. They can make your company more
productive, more profitable, and a better place for the people
who work and live there.

This book tells you how to make that happen. Let's get
started.

01

Look What We Can Do

At the ripe old age of 15, the Web has already changed human society so profoundly that historians have begun comparing the Internet Age with the Renaissance and the Industrial Revolution. The Web has connected nearly a billion people. With that many brains as its motivating force, the transformation forged by the Internet has morphed from quantitative to qualitative: The power of the collective "we" is nearly unfathomable. Each of those brains has some 10 billion neurons linked to one another through about 10,000 synapses. Now all that individual brainpower is tied together and amplified by the power of technology: The new and potent "we" is far smarter than any singular "me." For the first time, humans can act in mass collaboration, using the kind of collective intelligence once reserved for ants and bees—but now with human IQ driving the mix. The result is a quantum increase in the world's ability to conceive, create, compute, and connect. We are only beginning to comprehend the consequences.

"If at first the idea is not absurd, there is no hope for it."

—ALBERT EINSTEIN

Cyberwatchers say the Internet has evolved in two distinct stages: Web 1.0 and Web 2.0. In both of them, the Net has been a hugely fertile market where people turn data into money. But Web 1.0 winners profited (mainly in the dot-com boom) by cornering data for themselves and riding the price up. Web 2.0 innovators do the opposite. They believe information becomes more valuable as more people use it. Instead of  tightly controlling the code behind a new software program, for example, they let anyone alter or add to it, confident that the users will contribute their own ideas and improve the program for everyone. The miracle is that, by giving away access, the owners can actually reduce their own costs while winding up with a better product, certified as such by its volunteer creators—a product that can win ever more customers.

As a business model, that process is called open sourcing or *crowdsourcing*—it turns over tasks traditionally performed by employees to the Internet multitude. And it has claimed some memorable successes, particularly on the product-development front. Mozilla's Firefox open-source Web browser, for example, has been downloaded more than 300 million times and is used by an estimated 70 million to 80 million people. The Linux operating system, created as an open-source alternative to Windows and UNIX, can be downloaded free and altered to suit any user's needs; with all that firepower brought to bear, bugs in the system get fixed in a matter of hours. Some five million users per month swear by Wikipedia, the free online encyclopedia created and updated by Internet volunteers to the tune of two million articles and counting. Any visitor can edit *most* of its articles, although some, such as the entry on George W. Bush, are protected by volunteer administrators. That's because ideologues and mischief-makers occasionally take liberties with the facts, but the process is self-correcting as other users and administrators set them straight.

CROWDSOURCING

As of January 2006, open sourcing was, for most businesspeople, little more than an online curiosity. That was when Jeff Howe of *Wired* magazine started to write an article about the phenomenon. In his reporting, he discovered a far more important story to be told: Major companies in a variety of industries had begun farming out serious tasks to individuals and groups on the Internet. His editor at *Wired*, Mark Robinson, agreed. Together they coined a new word to describe the phenomenon. The article appeared in June of that year, and the word they invented, *crowdsourcing*, was defined as the tapping of the "latent talent of the [online] crowd"; it became the term of choice for a process that has been infiltrating virtually every aspect of business life.

Savvy companies are turning to the Internet hordes for help with new product development, customer service, sales, production, finance, and even management. They prosper by searching out, nurturing, and tapping the expertise of individual online communities, customers included.

The actual numbers of companies using online mass collaboration are surprising. Early in 2007, Forrester Research reported that a survey of 119 chief intelligence officers found that fully 89 percent were using at least one of six technologies for collective intelligence, including such unlikely business tools as podcasts, wikis, blogs, and social networking. A worldwide McKinsey & Company survey of 2,800 ranking executives found that the leading country in the trend was India, with 80 percent of its companies planning to increase their spending for online communities over the next three years. North America, with 65 percent planning increases, came in third, just behind companies in the Asia-Pacific region.

Naturally, there are pitfalls in crowdsourcing. If collaboration isn't done right, it had best not be done at all. Gartner Research has predicted, with 80 percent certainty, that by 2010, more than 60 percent of *Fortune* 1,000 companies will have some form of online community that can be used in marketing—but with the same degree of confidence, Gartner says half of those will be so poorly managed that they will do more harm than good.

"We're Going to Aggressively Expose Ourselves!"

Long before there was an Internet, of course, the power of mass collaboration was evident. From the hive of the honey bee to the barn-raisings of rural America, many communities have relied upon intense and all-but-universal cooperation. In the case of the honey bee, a system of signals, ranging from the release of a particular scent to the dance of a forager, triggers the crowd actions that keep the hive buzzing. Barn-raisings are inspired by a more conscious recognition of the benefits of mutual dependence.

Jeff Bezos, founder, chairman, and chief executive officer of Amazon.com, was thinking more about the benefits of a loyal customer base when he established Amazon's online customer reviews, which might have been the first clear example of business crowdsourcing. Done for no pay and with no controls by the company, they added real value to Amazon's offerings. They also inspired Bezos to take his business in a radical new direction.

During its first decade, the company had invested more than $2 billion to build and safeguard its giant database of proprietary information, including pricing, sales, customers, book reviews, and inventory data. In 2004, Bezos asked his senior management team a radical question: What if they opened the vault to public scrutiny so everyone could use the database?

Ever the contrarian, he advocated sharing Amazon's knowledge as a way of profiting even more from it. By letting savvy outsiders in, he argued, Amazon would enter into potentially profitable partnerships with them. Not all his colleagues were enthusiastic about the idea, but, in the end, Bezos prevailed. He ended the debate by opening his arms wide and declaring, "We're going to aggressively expose ourselves!"

The impact has been nothing short of phenomenal. Since Bezos made his bold move, more than 240,000 people have participated in what is now known as Amazon Web Services, and the number of software developers and entrepreneurs clamoring to join the crowd continues to grow at a rapid clip, up by more than 55 percent in the 12 months through January 2007. No longer a risky experiment, crowdsourcing is now a core part of Amazon's strategy. Collectively, the programmers and businesses that scurried to get a look at what Amazon knew have greatly expanded its knowledge and field of operations, developing hundreds of new shopping interfaces that have drawn millions of customers and vastly increased the company's sales and profits.

Independent entrepreneurs such as Daryl Butcher, Jason Meyer, and Hector Rivas, for instance, have sold millions of dollars' worth of used books since linking up with Amazon. Volume is the main strategic focus of their online Thrift Books venture—of necessity: How else could a company survive, let alone prosper, by selling books for as little as a penny? Instead of being bogged down in the time-wasting, money-losing tedium of cataloguing books by hand, Thrift Books has relied on Amazon's efficient technology to become one of the largest used-book sellers in the country, with revenues of more than $2.5 million a year.

Other innovative ideas also can find a welcoming and profitable home on Amazon. More than one million merchants, potential customers, showcase their wares, both new and used, on the site. ScoutPal, a technology that enables a cell phone or other wireless device to read bar codes, was one of those ideas that took flight after linking up with Amazon. It was born from one woman's problems in selling used books on the site.

Barbara Anderson shopped at yard and tag sales, but often found she paid more than she should have and couldn't recoup her investment, much less earn a profit. Her husband, Dave, experienced at writing software for wireless gadgets, stepped in to help. The program he came up with allowed Barbara to access Amazon's Web Services database using her cell phone. She could enter a book's bar code and instantly learn the price any given title was fetching on Amazon and how many copies were available for sale. With that information in hand, she was able to buy only those books she could profitably resell. The result: Her income rose threefold to $100,000, of which some 85 percent was profit. And there was a bonus: Her husband's

ScoutPal application has become a second Amazon-based family business, with more than 1,000 subscribers, each paying $10 a month.

Jeff Bezos has found yet another role for Amazon's huge community: In 2005, Bezos created a Web site to enroll volunteers in the task of finding duplicates among the millions of Amazon Web pages—a task that his software could not handle. The volunteers were given a few cents for each duplicate page they found. The process worked well, so Bezos turned it into a business. The Web site was renamed Mturk.com, and Amazon invited software developers to tap into it for such tasks as finding specific objects in photos, translating text, and judging the beauty of a scene or object.

The name of the service, Amazon Mechanical Turk, is a tongue-in-cheek homage to an eighteenth-century hoax in which a life-size mannequin, attired in a turban and robe, was able to take on all comers—and defeat most of them— in well-publicized chess matches. As was eventually discovered, a human chess master was hidden inside the "Mechanical Turk" machine.

Amazon has more than 100,000 so-called Turk workers today, in more than 100 countries. They are paid only pennies for their HITs (human intelligence tasks), and Bezos has been criticized for running a virtual sweatshop.

But the workers seem willing enough. Some see it as a kind of hobby, or a virtual jigsaw puzzle. One disabled veteran told a reporter that he could earn about $100 a week by working two hours a day for the Turk, and he called it "a form of therapy to get [him] used to working again."

The Turk's customers are satisfied, too. iConclude, a software company that sells automated programs to troubleshoot and repair information technology networks, posted a request on Mturk.com for one simple procedure and got replies from 300 programmers. Sunny Gupta, iConclude's CEO, says he got the job done for one-tenth what it would have cost in his own shop—and after the volunteers were paid, the Turk's fee was just an additional 10 percent.

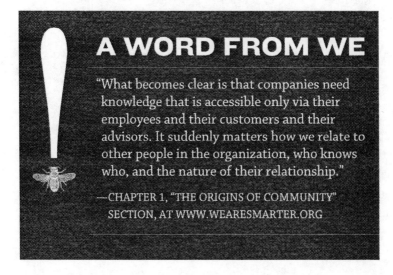

A WORD FROM WE

"What becomes clear is that companies need knowledge that is accessible only via their employees and their customers and their advisors. It suddenly matters how we relate to other people in the organization, who knows who, and the nature of their relationship."

—CHAPTER 1, "THE ORIGINS OF COMMUNITY" SECTION, AT WWW.WEARESMARTER.ORG

Amazon, of course, was just one of the pioneers in the crowdsourcing field. From the Internet telephone upstart Skype to eBay's massive auctions, new business models have sprung from online collaboration, and traditional companies such as Procter & Gamble, Hewlett-Packard, LEGO, and Eli Lilly are using communities in marketing, product development, customer relations, and even basic research and design. As some see it, the concentration of economic power that began in the Industrial Revolution is actually being reversed. University of Michigan business professor C. K. Prahalad has called the wikinomics trend "the democratization of industry," foreshadowing nothing less than "an economy of the people, by the people, and for the people."

Canada's Cambrian House entered the crowdsourcing lists in 2006 with a business premise that was simplicity itself: The best way to uncover new ideas for software and then pick the winners is to rely on software users themselves. That made for a somewhat startling offer when Cambrian's founder, Michael Sikorsky, was pitching the idea to his first investors. "We don't know what we're going to build, who

will build it, or who will buy what we make," he said. He raised $2.6 million anyway, and the pot has since grown to more than $8 million.

Sikorsky's model has worked so well that Cambrian House now has fully 30,000 community members dreaming up ideas, trying them out, collaborating on improvements, compensating each other for their time and work, and buying the final product. Those offerings have since grown beyond software to include entirely new businesses and even some physical goods. The company's guiding question (and answer): "How would you unleash the ideas, talents, and entrepreneurial drive of six billion people? Bring them together under one roof."

Here's how Cambrian House's crowdsourcing model works today.

A member of Cambrian's community—a student, an entrepreneur, a business advisor, an investor, a designer, or a game player—submits an idea. The community members rank it according to marketability and ease of distribution over the Internet. The feedback from the community helps the person who submitted the idea refine his or her concept and determine whether it merits becoming a commercial reality.

Cambrian House also helps highlight the community's hottest ideas in a tournament called IdeaWarz. Sixteen ideas compete head to head in four elimination rounds. Each week, the community votes to eliminate half of the IdeaWarz

contestants until a single champion is left. The winning proposal garners funding and fame. The contest is, in many ways, a filtering tool using the wisdom of crowds to determine the best idea in the community at that moment.

It also gives those who submit ideas the validation they need to feel confident that time and resources can now be dedicated to turning an idea into a business with the community's help.

They then connect with community members to write code for the program, develop a business plan, design a logo, and so on in exchange for royalty points or Cambros (Cambrian House's internal currency: One Cambros equals $1). Royalty points ensure a contributor shares in the product's profitability.

The Cambrian development community of programmers, graphic designers, copywriters, illustrators, and the like bring the concept to life. If it flops, well, better luck next time. If it takes off, the inventor and the members they worked with reap the rewards. As the builders of the platform responsible for helping its members connect and bring ideas to life, Cambrian House allows all those who submit ideas to maintain ownership of their intellectual property, but it plans to earn revenue by implementing minor transaction fees at some point (when royalties and Cambros are exchanged between members), and does invest in some ideas.

Determined to work with their community as partners, Cambrian House shares 1 percent of its annual profits with its community (a member co-op board determines how the funds are allocated).

To date, Cambrian House
has invested in four
crowdsourced products
that have come to the market. The first to produce revenues
was Prezzle.com, which enables you to send a friend online
greetings and gift certificates from vendors such as Amazon,
Bath & Body Works, and Sephora. You can choose your
wrapping paper, provide clues to what the gift is, and pick
the date it can be opened. Prezzle's revenues are modest—a
projected $1 million for 2008—but CEO Sikorsky hopes some
viral marketing and savvy business development partnership
will enable Prezzle to reach its tipping point.

Another of Cambrian's ventures, a desktop-to-desktop
combat game called Gwabs, started off as a big hit in
community forums, prompting the company to invest $8,000
in a market test. After selling hundreds of the games over
just one weekend, Cambrian poured another $100,000 into
developing the product for retail sale. All told, the company
spent only six months and $200,000 to turn the idea into a
marketable product, Sikorsky says, less than half the time and
a third of the cost of developing it in-house.

By harnessing the power of crowds, more businesspeople
can make—and are making—better decisions and bigger
profits. In mid-2006, for example, IBM invited its entire
community—employees, their family members, and
customers—to take part in a brainstorming session to
identify potential areas for innovation. In the first session
of the "innovation jam," fully 150,000 online volunteers
were given 72 hours to come up with ideas. They produced
46,000 suggestions, which the company's staffers sifted and
evaluated; then, in September, the online conclave assembled
again to vote on the ideas with the most potential.

BY HARNESSING THE POWER OF CROWDS, MORE BUSINESSPEOPLE CAN MAKE—AND ARE MAKING— BETTER DECISIONS AND BIGGER PROFITS.

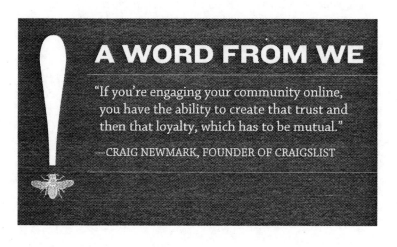

A WORD FROM WE

"If you're engaging your community online, you have the ability to create that trust and then that loyalty, which has to be mutual."

—CRAIG NEWMARK, FOUNDER OF CRAIGSLIST

IBM's CEO, Sam Palmisano, has promised to put as much as $100 million into developing the 10 winning ideas—and he will have a hand in the final choice.

The e.Lilly division of pharmaceutical giant Eli Lilly was among the first to harness the collaborative power of the Internet when in 2001 it launched Innocentive, the first online, incentive-based scientific network created specifically for the global research and development community. Innocentive's online platform allowed world-class scientists and R&D-based companies to collaborate to achieve innovative solutions to complex challenges. Innocentive offers "seeker companies" the opportunity to increase their R&D potential by posting challenges without violating their confidentiality and intellectual property interests. Seeker companies might be looking for a chemical to be used in art restoration, for instance, or the efficient synthesis of butane tetracarboxylic acid. David Bradin, a patent attorney from Seattle, was paid $4,000 for his tetracarboxylic acid formula. P&G says Innocentive has increased the share of its new products originating outside the company from 20 percent to 35 percent.

Though still in its infancy, crowdsourcing is already rewriting the rules of business, posing major challenges and opening up unprecedented opportunities. The chapters that follow address the specifics of the trend, from product development and marketing to production, financing, management techniques, and even strategy. Coming up:

❖ Chapter 2, "Go from R&D to R&WE," shows how to use communities to spot new market opportunities, identify benefits, and sharpen new products and services. Among the pioneering companies featured: Brewtopia, Idea Crossing, General Mills, Kraft, Linden Lab, and Procter & Gamble.

❖ Chapter 3, "How May We Help We?", shows how to make use of communities to improve service and increase customer satisfaction. Among the businesses featured: Bradbury Software, Cookshack, Intuit, and PMI Audio Group.

❖ Chapter 4, "Customer, Sell Thyself," provides insights into the use of community-based techniques to reduce selling and marketing costs while boosting customer loyalty. Cases in point: MasterCard, Nike, and the Portland Trailblazers.

❖ Chapter 5, "If We Build It, We Will Come," shares lessons about how communities are changing methods and best practices in factories, virtual and otherwise, around the world. Companies whose experiences are detailed include: iStockphoto, Reevoo, ThisNext, and Zebo.

❖ Chapter 6, "Welcome to the World Bank of We," explains how to tap communities to help fund business growth and support worthy charitable causes. Prosper is one of the primary examples cited.

❖ Chapter 7, "Make Everyone a C-We-O," sheds
light on how to use communities to organize and
manage companies. The centerpiece case study:
TheBusinessExperiment.com.

❖ Chapter 8, "Lead from the Rear," details some of the key
lessons we learned in the course of our experiment with
wearesmarter.org.

We'll start at the beginning: What are you going to sell? Years
ago, the late, lamented Packard luxury car came up with a
classic slogan, "Ask the man who owns one." These days,
some of the country's leading corporations are doing just that,
asking their own customers for help in creating new products
and services and improving old ones. The chapter just ahead
explores that trend, describing the impressive results these
organizations are achieving and how they go about it—and
how you can, too.

02

Go from R&D to R&We

Back in the Aussie summer of 2002, Liam Mulhall was ready
to abandon the high-stress, high-tech business. He had put
in his time at the local office of Red Hat, the big U.S.-based
provider of open sourcing solutions, and now he and his
two buddies had a new Plan A. They wanted to buy a pub in
Sydney. The problem was, the price was more than the lads
could afford. So they fell back on Plan B, which, in this case,
was Plan Brew. With a nothing-to-lose attitude—"It was our
money and not a lot of it," Mulhall allows—they would make
beer, but with a twist; they were going to tap the power of
community.

Mulhall had stumbled onto the story of PK-35, a Finnish
soccer club. The team's coach invited fans to determine its
recruiting, training, and even game
tactics by allowing them to vote
using their cell phones. The idea
put the fizz in Mulhall's lager. As he
would later write, he had found "the
best way to run a business—give the
customers the reins."

"Innovation is simply group intelligence having fun."
—MICHAEL NOLAN

Luckily, Mulhall and his two friends didn't know that the 2002 soccer season would be so disastrous that PK-35 would fire its coach and scrap its fan-driven ways. So they went ahead with their scheme, setting up a Web site, Brewtopia. com.au, and inviting 140 of their friends to describe their ideal beer. Within weeks, the community had built up a head of more than 10,000 people in 20 countries, and their votes determined everything from the beer's style (lager), color (pale amber), and alcohol content (4.5 percent) to the shape of the bottle and the colors printed on the label.

The founders, however, were—and are—solely responsible for the beer's name. For reasons comprehensible only to an Australian (let's just say it has to do with sheep), they called it Blowfly.

Chief executive and "spokesmodel" Mulhall and pals, Greg Bunt and Larry Hedges, contracted with a brewery to make and bottle their concoction. But how to sell it? As the Brewtopia site explains, "In Australia there is a 'brewing duopoly,' two major brewers who have contracts with most outlets and bars that restrict the smaller boutique beers. If you don't have the bucks to throw at retailers, you just don't get exposure." The solution: Blowfly would be sold in direct shipments through the Web site, beginning with the people who helped design the beer, and, thus, would have what Mulhall calls "viral equity" (a.k.a. shares in the company) and a predilection to try the brew. And in line with the company's crowdsourcing origins, the site would enable members of the Blowfly community to customize the label on the bottle, choosing a template from among a dozen offered, typing in their own text, and uploading their own photos or artwork.

Four years later, in 2007, with, as Mulhall would have it, "no brewing experience, no industry experience, no marketing experience, no money, and no idea what [they] were doing," Brewtopia had 50,000 customers in 46 nations. Having already branched out to wine and bottled water, soft drinks were on the way, Mulhall told London-based marketing consultant Johnnie Moore. Brewtopia also sells brand-promoting T-shirts and caps.

Mulhall and his buddies give Brewtopia a wisecracking zest that appeals to their young customers, further reinforcing the sense of community. "Some people think this is a cheap publicity stunt," the Web site proclaims. "Well, there's nothing cheap about it!" If customers don't like the beer, the message adds, "you're in desperate need of a taste bud transplant—but we'd rather not foot the bill for that—instead we'll gladly refund your money in return for the unused beer as long as you give us your feedback on what didn't 'work for you.'"

In his telephone interview with Moore, conducted, fittingly enough, via Skype, Mulhall declared that a business has to constantly keep moving, reinventing itself "like Madonna." For Brewtopia, which is now flush with cash from its initial public offering on Australia's National Stock Exchange, the next move is into retail. "Unless you drop your stuff in a shop, people don't believe you are a real company," he said. As for Mulhall himself, he just might have a go at the financial industry, specifically community banking, where giving customers a voice in how the business is run could be a differentiating feature with great appeal (more on this topic later in the book).

The Community Is Always Right

For businesses large and small, in Australia and elsewhere, it's no inconsequential decision to let customers dictate what is sold. New product development is among the most important activities any enterprise undertakes. A  business lives or dies on the strength of what it offers, and it's understandable that leaders often resist losing control over the basic nature of the goods they sell.

But there's much to be said for tapping the collective wisdom of a community—customer or otherwise—for product ideas and improvements. In the case of customers, it gives them a vested interest in the results and all but guarantees they will like—and buy—what they've created. You might even be able to skip the whole test-marketing process (but, of course, that's up to you).

Imagine the computers that Acer or Gateway or Hewlett-Packard could create with input from customers— computers made not for geeks who love to install memory cards and new software, but for the rest of us, who like to drive cars without having to know how to repair the fuel injector.

In the pages that follow are a host of examples of innovative organizations that, like Brewtopia, have pioneered product development by people not on their payroll. These businesses range from food giants to the inventors of a popular virtual world that has confounded skeptics who believed only

nerds would sign on. These organizations' commitment
to the collaborative process ranges from cautious to total
immersion.

Nikoli

Maki Kaji likes to
bet on the ponies,
which explains why,
when he started a
puzzle magazine in
1980, he named it
Nikoli in honor of a
winning racehorse.
The quarterly
magazine, based in

Tokyo, turned out to be a good bet, too. It offers some 30
different types of puzzles with each issue, and a third of them
are brand new. They are the handiwork not of the company's
employees, but of its readers.

Kaji is the world's most prolific pencil-
and-paper puzzle creator, and he
publishes them by the hundreds in
Nikoli and in all sorts of books and
other puzzle magazines. But he relies
on others to do the creating. In the
case of Sudoku, for example, which
Kaji promoted around the globe, the
inventor was an American. For the rest,
he looks to his tens of thousands of
subscribers.

They submit their ideas for new kinds of puzzles, a staff of
20 goes through them, and the most promising appear in the
next issue of *Nikoli*. Readers then send in their reactions and
critiques. Out of that process, Kaji has winnowed some 250
new kinds of puzzles, which get printed in his books.

In the case of Sudoku, he trademarked the game in Japan but
nowhere else, so he receives no royalties from the huge sales
of the game around the world. He claims to be unfazed, and
he has no intention of trademarking other new games. "This
openness is more in keeping with *Nikoli's* open culture," he
told the *New York Times*. "We're prolific because we do it for
the love of the games, not the money." He prides himself on
never having advertised *Nikoli*, letting the Japanese love of
mathematics and games do the selling.

Working a puzzle is like being at the
track, he explains: "Not just the fun of **nikoli**
solving it, but the excitement before,
even if you don't solve it. It's that
excitement before the finish line when the horses are roaring
down the stretch and you're cheering them on."

Nikoli first published a complicated version of Sudoku in
1984. Its readers offered their modifications and corrections
until Kaji had a puzzle he thought was a winner, and it caught
on in Japan. But it wasn't until the *London Times* picked it up
20 years later that Sudoku took off. And that put Kaji and his
company in the spotlight as puzzle promoters. Lately, another
community-provided numbers puzzle from *Nikoli*, called
Kakuro, has been taking the world by storm.

WHAT YOU CAN DO

❖ **The medium is not the message.**
Before the Internet and e-mail invaded our lives, Maki Kaji was tapping the talent of his magazine community by snail mail. A company's goal is to convince us, as the necessary "we," to take part; the means of communication, important though it be, is secondary.

❖ **Know your neighbors.** Because Kaji identified with his readers and understood them so well, he knew he could count on them to join the game-invention game.

Procter & Gamble

For generations, the research and development (R&D) team at Procter & Gamble, 9,000-strong, had been the stuff of business legend, cranking out dozens of high-profile, high-profit new products year after year. But in 2000, A. G. Lafley, the company's newly arrived chairman and chief executive officer, stunned his prideful researchers. They were not, he announced, producing winners

A WORD FROM WE

"One of the main reasons that people get involved as a community participant for a company is because of the pain they experience with the product or the service. In the pain-solving process, the company learns so much about how to make their products better."

—DENISE HOWELL, BLOGGER

big enough or fast enough to significantly boost corporate revenues. His solution was drastic: By the end of the decade, fully half of all new P&G products and technologies would have to come from outside the company.

The object, Lafley insisted, was not to supplant the mighty in-house R&D effort, but to supplement it. That turned out to be a vastly difficult venture, though, and no wonder, given the company's size and complexity. For one thing, the internal communication systems had to be reinvented to make it possible for all parts of the company to exchange data and brainstorm. Then that information had to be made available to noncompany entities, including suppliers and distributors.

Another stumbling block was the resistance of many of P&G's key researchers. Some complained that the proposed changes in their way of doing things would stifle creativity. Others feared a loss of power and prestige if their information and work had to be shared.

Lafley persevered. His most drastic move was a giant step
into crowdsourcing. P&G put together a global community
made up of high-tech entrepreneurs
and open networks such as NineSigma,   ***P&G***
and including the retired scientists
and engineers of YourEncore and the
marketplace for intellectual property exchange called Yet2.
com. P&G has also gone to Innocentive, a network of 120,000
self-selected technical people from more than 175 countries
who receive cash awards if their ideas prove out.

In seeking help from its extended community, P&G submits
so-called "science problems" for solutions. Sometimes the
problems come from in-house R&D, representing blind
alleys those researchers have come up against. Sometimes
the company asks its online partners for help in adapting
a feature of a competitor's product to one of its own. The
right answers have greatly benefited P&G. In the case of
Innocentive, for example, a third of the dozens of problems
posed have been solved. One crisp example of an early
crowdsourcing triumph: When the company was stymied
for a way to print messages on its Pringles potato chips, the
development community found a bakery in Italy with a little-
publicized process that could do the job.

P&G is closing in on Lafley's goal. As of 2006, the company
was deriving 35 percent of its ideas from outsiders.
Meanwhile, R&D productivity has soared 60 percent. A
whopping 80 percent of its product launches are successful,
compared to 30 percent for the consumer-products industry

as a whole. And it spends 3.1 percent, or
about $2.1 billion, of its more than $68
billion in annual worldwide revenue on
research and development, much more
than others in the industry.

WHAT YOU CAN DO

❖ **Tread firmly but carefully.** Seeking the help of outsiders, even when they're part of some amorphous, unseen community, can be threatening to in-house staff. They will resist. Make your intentions clear, as P&G's Lafley did, and stick to them. Meanwhile, do everything possible to accommodate the concerns of the resisters. For example, P&G allowed researchers to type up their notes in Microsoft Word or continue to rely on an older system that was modified to make it compatible with the new pilot technology.

❖ **Thank you for sharing.** Ironically, some of the same companies that have seen the crowdsourcing light and reached outside their walls have overlooked the wealth of intelligence and experience in the nontechnical side of their operations. The days of kissing off employees' ideas with a couple of suggestion boxes is long past. No business can afford to ignore the ideas and inside knowledge brewing in the minds of its accountants and lawyers, production line, and sales crew, just waiting for management to provide an incentive to join in.

Linden Lab

General Motors has created a whole complex where you can
go to a drive-in theater or a tune-up shop and, oh yes, check
out the Pontiac Solstice. Dell has a factory where you can
customize your PC and have it shipped to your door. Reuters
has set up a newsroom to help you keep up with what's going
on in the world. And you can enjoy it all without moving an
inch from your office desk or your easy chair.

You're in Second Life, the online virtual universe. Some
people are still calling it a game, but they don't include GM,
Dell, Reuters, and dozens of other corporations. They see this
ultimate example of crowdsourcing as strictly business.

The handiwork of Linden Lab, a San Francisco–based 3D
entertainment company, Second Life has been and is being
shaped entirely by its five million or so members. They are
represented by cartoonlike avatars who can go to casinos, sex
clubs, and shopping malls; attend concerts (Suzanne Vega
and Duran Duran have performed there); design furniture;
invent weapons; and drive cars. They can also devise alternate
lifestyles, make new friends, start new careers, and adopt a
new personality.

Second Lifers can also get
their virtual flu shots from
a virtual employee of the Centers
for Disease Control and Prevention; bump into
House Speaker Nancy Pelosi and other political types
on Capitol Hill island; and attend college-level lectures
in virtual classrooms provided by the likes of Harvard,
Ohio University, the Australian Film TV and Radio School,
and New York University.

All sorts of companies have joined the crowd—for all sorts of reasons. Some are pitching or testing products. Starwood Hotels plans to open its new prototype, The Aloft, in 2008, and has built a virtual version in Second Life to get members' feedback on its design and features. It has sponsored concerts there to bring in visitors, most recently featuring Ben Folds, formerly the lead singer of the now-defunct Ben Folds Five.

Other companies are using Second Life as a meeting place where employees and managers from around the country or the world can gather away from the office while still sitting at their desks. At one virtual IBM session, avatars representing researchers in Australia, Florida, India, and Ireland hashed over supercomputing problems, instant messages bouncing back and forth. Thousands of IBM employees now have routine meetings on the site.

Advanced Micro Devices prides itself on being "a leading global provider of innovative processing solutions in the computing, graphics, and consumer electronics markets." In other words, it lives or dies by software developers. So it has created a pavilion in Second Life where developers, new and old, can network and attend lectures and training courses. It's located on the Second Life Developer Archipelago, and it includes an exhibition hall with interactive booths, scripted banners, and streaming videos.

Meanwhile, Linden Lab is not slowing down. In addition to instant messaging, the company now offers members the option of actually speaking to each other, using computer headsets. Not content with having established a virtual world built by the crowd, Linden has taken its crowdsourcing a step further.

WHAT YOU CAN DO

❖ **Get serious about the crowd.** When open sourcing first appeared, it was greeted mostly as a curiosity, certainly nothing that had a practical dollars-and-cents significance. When Second Life opened for business, hard-headed businesspeople had pretty much the same reaction. No longer. The notion that the Internet crowds represent an important potential value beyond their role as customers has finally penetrated many corporate heads. How about yours?

❖ **Ask the right question.** If ever there was an example of the need to innovate these days, it has to be Second Life. The activities that some companies have undertaken are fascinating and make it clear that leaders have to find a way to expand their view of the possible. There are so many ways you haven't thought of to leverage your online community. One approach is to expand the universe of people you're depending upon for new ideas. Include everyone in the company, or all of your stakeholders (including investors), or all of your customers. One of your competitors might be taking those steps at this very moment. The question no longer is "What will they think of next?", but rather "How much time do we have before they think of it?"

It has released the code of its viewer application so that the online community of developers can improve it or add new features. No doubt, Second Life will be unrecognizable within another year or two.

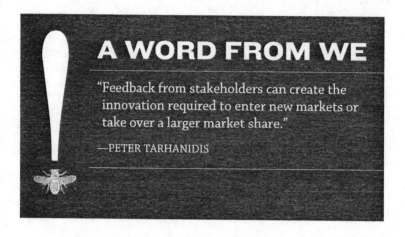

A WORD FROM WE

"Feedback from stakeholders can create the innovation required to enter new markets or take over a larger market share."

—PETER TARHANIDIS

SugarCRM

This start-up in Cupertino, California, uses the power of community to create and continuously improve its open-source customer relationship management (CRM) software. Founder and CEO John Roberts describes it as "the collective work of bright CRM engineers around the world."

Before Roberts came along, open-source product development was limited to the infrastructure side of the IT market. Betting that a growing number of individual users and IT managers were fed up with having to pay big licensing fees for proprietary applications designed to help manage sales and keep tabs on customers, Roberts and his company offered customers free software, but with real people and their cache of knowledge standing by for support.

More than one million companies or individuals have downloaded the software since the company released its first version in April 2004, and any one of them can pitch in

to patch holes, fix errors, provide more elegant programming, or build third-party extensions. The open-source product refinements and extensions take place in what the company calls the SugarForge. Here interested parties can see what kind of functionality Sugar has

to offer at any given time. Sugar earns revenue by providing technical support and customized versions of its software.

Some critics say Sugar's business model is confusing and failure prone because it offers both an on-demand subscription version of its software and the option of having the program installed on in-house networks; either option allows for customer modifications. Others scoff at the notion that a significant number of corporate software buyers will take a flyer on unknown open-source CRM applications.

But fans of Sugar counter that it is precisely the business customers who are clamoring for less expensive choices that can be customized to their particular needs and wants. And even if the purchasing executives themselves aren't savvy about open sourcing, their IT departments certainly are. Good reviews for Sugar will filter up, they say.

Given that paying customers have migrated to Sugar over the past three years—all without any big and expensive corporate marketing campaigns—the proponents of the sweeter view seem to have the edge.

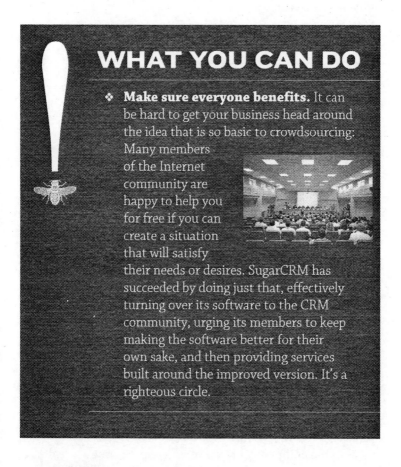

WHAT YOU CAN DO

❖ **Make sure everyone benefits.** It can be hard to get your business head around the idea that is so basic to crowdsourcing: Many members of the Internet community are happy to help you for free if you can create a situation that will satisfy their needs or desires. SugarCRM has succeeded by doing just that, effectively turning over its software to the CRM community, urging its members to keep making the software better for their own sake, and then providing services built around the improved version. It's a righteous circle.

Virgin Mobile USA

The cell phone company uses 2,000 carefully selected online customers—"Insiders," as Virgin calls them—to keep it abreast of trends and promising opportunities. Virgin describes the group as "a team of elite,

Sir Richard Branson, founder and chairman of the Virgin Group, shows one of the first cell phones available from the leading U.S. wireless youth network Virgin Mobile USA.

young, and active customers," and it
rewards them with free calling minutes
and phone upgrades.

A joint venture of Richard Branson's
Virgin Group and Sprint Nextel, the
company goes to its Insider community—think: very hip
focus group—for help on everything from designing phones
to coming up with names for service plans. As one officer of
the company put it, "Ultimately, what we want to do is put
young consumers backstage."

But this is not high school, and being accepted as part of the
in-crowd is not the only way to be heard and earn rewards
at Virgin Mobile USA. The company, whose pay-as-you-go,
no-contract service has attracted 4.6 million phone users,
offers all of its mostly young Chatty Cathys and Texter
Thomases the chance to earn free phone minutes simply by
paying attention and giving feedback on a corporate sponsor's
advertisement. Any Virgin Mobile customer who watches
30-second commercials on his or her computer screen,
reads text messages on a cell phone, or fills out brand survey
questionnaires can earn up to 75 minutes a month of free
airtime. Called Sugar Mama, the program gives a notoriously
voluble group the chance to stay one step ahead of a dead cell
phone by voicing their opinions.

But more to the point, Sugar Mama enables sponsoring
partners to tap into the thoughts and opinions of a coveted
marketing segment, and they're happy to pay for the privilege.
As one corporate media director pointed out, knowing that
the kids don't get paid unless they watch an ad and answer
questions helps assure advertisers that they are getting
honest feedback.

THIS IS NOT HIGH SCHOOL, AND BEING ACCEPTED AS PART OF THE IN-CROWD IS NOT THE ONLY WAY TO BE HEARD AND EARN REWARDS.

Catering to the crowd has also delivered an unexpected benefit to Virgin Mobile: buzz marketing. The kids are talking about the company, even those who use another network. When the company kicked off a clever text-messaging marketing program called Adopt-A-Mime that featured silent mimics in whiteface, the word spread fast, both in and out of the Virgin Mobile network. The buzz caused a notable number of non-Virgin customers to inquire about adopting a mime.

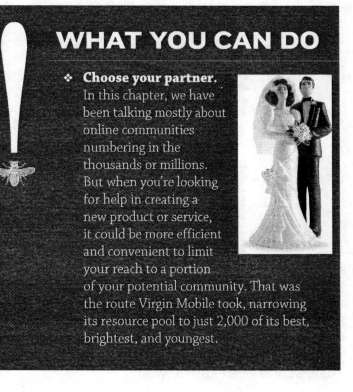

WHAT YOU CAN DO

❖ **Choose your partner.** In this chapter, we have been talking mostly about online communities numbering in the thousands or millions. But when you're looking for help in creating a new product or service, it could be more efficient and convenient to limit your reach to a portion of your potential community. That was the route Virgin Mobile took, narrowing its resource pool to just 2,000 of its best, brightest, and youngest.

WHAT YOU CAN DO

❖ **Spread the joy.** While concentrating on its Insider group, Virgin Mobile had the good sense not to deprive its other customers of a way to earn a reward. Had it not designed the Sugar Mama program for the masses, the bulk of its customers might have become resentful, thereby negating the Insider group's impact on product development. As it is, satisfaction surveys, such as those conducted by J. D. Power and Associates among wireless pre-paid customers and those conducted by Virgin Mobile USA among its own customers, put Virgin Mobile at the top of the heap.

❖ **Think almost free.** Sometimes you might actually want to pay the members of your community—not because they would otherwise refuse to help, but because it's a way to make them more committed to your cause. Free minutes and phone upgrades will not dent Virgin Mobile's bottom line, but they work wonders in convincing the company's young customers to go "backstage." Of course, you need to be careful not to insult sophisticated volunteer members of your community with trinkets.

Idea Crossing

Fresh strategic ideas from fresh-faced MBA students—that's the product marketed by Idea Crossing, a Los Angeles start-up. Each year it runs the Innovation Challenge, a contest that tosses corporate problems into the laps of 3,000 of the brightest minds on college campuses around the world. Organizations ranging from the U.S. Postal Service to Hilton Hotels and Whirlpool pay $50,000 and up to sponsor the brain-bending competitions among school teams.

Founded in 2002 by Anil Rathi, then a gifted innovator himself at the Thunderbird School of Global Management, Idea Crossing initially hoped to link consumers who had come up with great product ideas to the companies that could bring the ideas to market. The competition started as something of an incidental experiment. But when the brainiacs leaped at the chance to tackle real-world problems and the companies swooned over the solutions these young outsiders came up with, the "experiment" graduated into the annual Innovation Challenge.

In the 2006 competition, a team from the Desautels Faculty of Management at McGill University in Montreal beat out 439 other teams of graduate students from 88 universities for top honors and a $20,000 prize. Its winning ideas centered on growth-enhancing partnerships for Hilton Hotels and ways to connect Chrysler with baby boomers. The strategic details are not for public consumption; they now become the intellectual property of the competition's sponsors.

The Bronfman Building, home of the
Desautels Faculty of Management.

WHAT YOU CAN DO

❖ **Decide who does what.** The scenario
is familiar. Your company recognizes a
promising new business idea, which you
adopt and develop.
Then along come the
entrepreneurs who have
sniffed out a new market.
They develop a different
spin on the idea, which
they offer to share with
you for a fee. Fair enough.
But the danger is that,
before you know it, you're relying entirely
on the entrepreneurs for new takes
on the idea—and you're starting to lose
your company's innovative chops for lack
of practice.

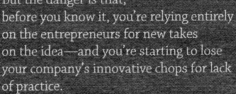

Business has only begun to tap
the infinite potential of online
communities as arbiters and creators
of new designs and products.
Variations on Second Life are popping
up all over, for example, offering
untold opportunities for companies
to interact with creative consumers in
new and different ways.

But the contributions of crowdsourcing to the bottom line
are by no means limited to product development. In the next
chapter, we describe how companies are using communities
to handle their customer service needs—and the risks and
rewards of that approach. We also explore the reasons so
many customers are so happy to help each other, for free.

03

How May We Help We?

Hokie 15 of Tigard, Oregon, had a question: "I just got my new Smokette. It seems a bit small. Has anyone sent theirs back to upgrade?"

So did Vizguy of Hunt$Vega$, otherwise known as Huntsville, Alabama: "Can I use the Cookshack smoker in my garage without posing a problem?"

JPSmokin of Boise, Idaho, meanwhile, was having a blast: "Thanks to everyone for all the advice, recommendations, and recipes," he wrote. "Picked up my new 008 smoker oven Saturday, and it hasn't been setting idle. Shoot, I haven't had this much fun since the boss's wife lost her swimsuit top at the company picnic."

"Clean up your own mess."
—ROBERT FULGHUM

Hour by hour, day by day, hundreds of online Cookshack customers sign onto its various forums to ask and answer questions about barbecue sauce (another product line), smoker and barbecue ovens, and cooking techniques. All this Internet jabber seems to work fine for all parties, but it does seem a tad incongruous, given the down-home subject and the fact that we're talking about an old-fashioned, low-tech kind of business.

For more than 40 years, Cookshack has been cranking out ovens for home and commercial use in a 21,000-square-foot factory in Ponca City, Oklahoma. It was founded by Gene Ellis, a businessman and inventor, and his wife, Judy. Gene got his inspiration watching neighbors try to turn old refrigerators into barbecue smokers. He built a cabinet and added a tray to hold smoldering wood chips, and Judy helped develop recipes for the company's sauces and meat rubs. After the Ellises' deaths in a 1985 boating accident, their son and daughter took over. The major claim they make for their company is that its machines make barbecue and smoked foods "without a lot of fuss." That's because the food is wood-cooked at a low temperature under static conditions with no through movement of air (which tends to dry meat) and no need for water pans (moisture stays in the oven).

Buyers of the ovens and smokers, which range from a model that holds 25 pounds of meat to one that can handle as much as 750 pounds, get a 30-day money-back guarantee and the promise of great after-  purchase support. (The Cookshack Web site proclaims that "the customer is [almost] always right.") Cookshack has 25 employees and actively encourages its customers to contact the company (its toll-free number appears prominently on every page of its Web site). The forums are an adjunct to its live customer service and are meant to provide a body of knowledge that couldn't be transmitted in a phone call and to provide assistance 24 hours a day, seven days a week. And they are clearly popular. A recent visit to the cooking-technique section revealed 1,196 topics and 10,126 posts. By creating a folksy, friendly site and designing forums and archives tailored to all tastes, the company has sold its customers on providing their own customer support.

All sorts of businesses are transferring much of the service function onto the shoulders of the customers themselves. Traditionally, of course, customers who had questions about a product—how to put it together, why it wasn't working properly, how to use it to the best advantage—would call the company's help line and talk with a customer service representative.

"All of our service representatives are helping other customers, but your call is very important to us. Please stay on the line. Your waiting time is approximately 32 minutes."

That's still possible, but it's not as easy as it used to be. Getting through to a service representative can take 30 minutes or more, and even then, customers are liable to get shifted from one level of expertise to another. Meanwhile, under pressure

to reduce costs, many businesses have begun charging substantial fees for telephone support. After the warranty on Dell computers expires, for instance, the company collects $39 for each tech support call unless the customer has paid $189 for a one-year service contract. Apple iMac customers get to purchase a three-year version for $169.

The alternative these companies offer is a visit to their online version of customer service. Typically, there is a FAQ page 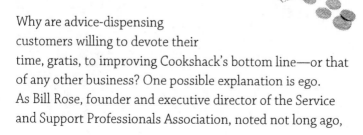 and probably one or more forums where customers can pose a question and have it answered by others who volunteer their time and wisdom. Hokie 15, for example, was assured by Cookshack forum gurus that he could prepare all sorts of wonderful barbecue on his Smokette, and they even gave him some recipes to try. Vizguy was warned that he might be smoking himself along with his brisket if he cooked in the garage.

For companies that offer it, online support has been a double boon. They save money by freeing customer-service personnel for other work, while also building a cohesive, loyal community of repeat customers who can be tapped for other purposes—say, to test new products.

Why are advice-dispensing customers willing to devote their time, gratis, to improving Cookshack's bottom line—or that of any other business? One possible explanation is ego. As Bill Rose, founder and executive director of the Service and Support Professionals Association, noted not long ago,

"Most customers want to be seen as experts and recognized as gurus in their fields." We suspect that a number of people in customer-service communities simply enjoy interacting with other like-minded individuals and helping them solve their problems.

If you're a barbecue enthusiast, like the crowd that hangs out at the Cookshack site, what better way to pass the time than exchanging experiences and suggestions with fellow smokemeisters? (By the way, you don't need a cast of thousands to advise customers online. Just 1 or 2 percent of the customer base can handle the job, according to Ron Munz, chief executive officer of the Help Desk Institute, an information technology trade association.)

Shifting service to a customer community raises some interesting questions, though. For one—and this is a biggie—how can you be sure that customers will provide the right answers? Suppose that, instead of elaborating on the Smokette's virtues, someone tells Hokie 15 that his oven is too small and then recommends a competitor's product? Can you trust your community to send defective product cases or billing problems directly to your service representatives rather than trying to deal with the customers online? In fact, where should the line be drawn between the two kinds of customer service?

Those are among the questions addressed by the following examples.

Netflix

Along with its inviting online presentation and oh-so-efficient distribution system, this booming movie-rental company prides itself on its capability to offer subscribers a compact list of films they are likely to enjoy watching.

"Imagine that our Web site was a brick-and-mortar store," Netflix vice president James Bennett told the *Los Angeles Times*. "When people walk through the door, they see the DVDs rearrange themselves. The movies that might interest them fly onto the shelves, and all the rest go to the back room."

In the real world, the movies don't do the rearranging; that's handled by the customers themselves, with an assist from a computer program called Cinematch. Customers are invited to rate each Netflix film they watch on a scale from 1 to 5. Cinematch digests these ratings, searches through the 80,000 titles in inventory, and comes up with a list of films tailored to the taste of each of the company's six million subscribers. By enticing them to rate films, Netflix achieves the latest in business magic tricks, getting customers to serve themselves.

The use of so-called recommenders is hardly unique to Netflix. Other online retailers, such as Amazon, Apple, eBay, and Overstock, rely on their customers for a helping hand in predicting what products the customers will prefer, whether bedding, books, CDs, or DVDs.

Customer ratings are used to rank corporate service providers as well.

For all these companies, the recommender system offers
more than the chance to provide an extra service. It helps
them establish a stronger connection with customers. Studies
have shown that it can substantially increase online sales.

The extent of Netflix's commitment to personalized movie
recommendations was made clear in November 2006 when
the company offered a
$1 million prize—in true
wikinomics spirit—to
anyone who can build
a system that is at least
10 percent better at the
job than Cinematch. The
competition is to end in
2011. Meanwhile, Netflix has enticed many of the leading
lights in the field of artificial intelligence to join in. Among
the contestants' discoveries to date: For reasons unknown,
most Netflix subscribers share the same attitude toward *The
Wizard of Oz* and *Silence of the Lambs*.

The company has made yet another bow to crowdsourcing
with a feature called Friends. It enables subscribers to see
each other's list of films watched, to compare the ratings
they have awarded the films, and to exchange suggestions for
other films to watch. Once again, the crowd is invited to play
a role in customer service.

Bradbury Software

In his office in Nashville,
Tennessee, home of the
Grand Ole Opry, Nick
Bradbury was a one-man
band. The company's
only employee, he sort of
liked the solitary life.

WHAT YOU CAN DO

❖ **Save!** On average, telephone customer support costs a company $25 to $50 a call; even e-mails run $4 to $15 per contact. That should be enough to inspire you to consider getting your company's community to take on part of the support job. As Netflix discovered with its recommender program, a community's services are often virtually free.

❖ **Promote!** Even though its personalized recommendations are so important in the Netflix scheme of things, they are not promoted on the company's "Welcome" and "How It Works" pages. So unless you go deeper into the site and become a member, you never learn about the rating system and the part it plays in nominating films you'll really like. That goes for the Friends feature as well. If you want your customers to serve themselves and you want potential customers to know about the value that creates, make sure you let them know up front and personal.

WHAT YOU CAN DO

❖ **Reward!** Netflix's decision to offer a prize for a system that outmatches Cinematch is a reminder that rewards are potent energizers for customers engaged in service and support functions. One effective approach is to have customers rank those customers who help them, and then award them special status of some kind—a symbol next to their icon, for example—and/or small items bearing the company logo.

After graduating from the University of Tennessee, he tried to make a living as a cartoonist. His comic strip, about a koala bear named Basil, poked fun at everything from politicians to television commercials. Then Bradbury took up computer programming, another solitary occupation, eventually creating the HTML editor, Homesite, which he sold in 1996. Two years later, he founded Bradbury Software and all by himself developed FeedDemon, a news aggregator, and TopStyle, a Web design program.

Bradbury's products were selling well, but he had a problem. When it came to customer support, his company was off-

key. There was no way he could keep up with customers' questions and occasional complaints, so

he handed over the job to the customers themselves. On
the Bradbury Web site, he set up a customer-to-customer
forum, a so-called peer support group where more than 2,000
people provided the after-purchase service he couldn't handle
himself.

In May 2005, Bradbury Software was acquired by NewsGator
Technologies, based in Denver, and Nick Bradbury was
hired and given the title "Architect,
Client Products." In other words,
he continues to spend hours alone,
thinking about new ways to improve
his two products. He also regularly
visits the forums on the NewsGator
Web site to check out product
suggestions his customers offer.

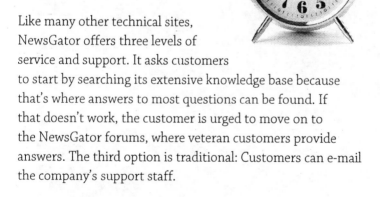

Like many other technical sites,
NewsGator offers three levels of
service and support. It asks customers
to start by searching its extensive knowledge base because
that's where answers to most questions can be found. If
that doesn't work, the customer is urged to move on to
the NewsGator forums, where veteran customers provide
answers. The third option is traditional: Customers can e-mail
the company's support staff.

To make sure the Bradbury products' customer service is
properly maintained, NewsGator decided to hire a new
customer service manager. It started by looking close to home
and found just the right person: Jack Brewster, a customer
who had been a major contributor on the original Bradbury
forums. You can take the boy out of the Bradbury, but you
can't take the Bradbury out of the boy.

WHAT YOU CAN DO

❖ **Ride herd.** The benefits of turning over a portion of the service function to customers are substantial, but so are the dangers. Those expert customers could be handing out inexpert answers. Follow  Nick Bradbury's example and make sure you "check out" your customer forums on a regular basis.

❖ **Get organized.** As the NewsGator approach suggests, a high-traffic support Web site should give the customer-in-need more than a single option. Questions and answers should be analyzed and organized in an archive or  knowledge base. Many customers prefer using such a system—the same folks who would rather use an ATM than deal with a bank teller. That's good news because it means that your customers who man the forums have more time to deal with problems. By the way, those volunteers should be encouraged to become experts in navigating the archive so they can use it to make sure they're handing out the right skinny.

PMI Audio Group

Around the same time Nick Bradbury began his solitary life as a computer programmer in Tennessee, Alan Hyatt, one-time professional guitarist, was setting up PMI Audio Group, a California-based distributor of professional audio equipment. He called his company a group, but, like Bradbury, he was the only employee. Today PMI is still a distributor, handling recording, video, film, broadcast, and other products. But now it owns most of the businesses whose products it sells. That means PMI must concern itself with matters most distributors don't have to worry about: product design, manufacturing, marketing, and customer service.

To cope with customer service, the company relies, in part, on its online forums where old hands instruct newbies on the intricacies of such complex topics as multipattern diaphragm condensers, dual-channel mic, precompressor EQ, and ATB mixers. The discussions of technical issues turned out to be so detailed and to the point that the company archived them on its Web site, organized according to product, and directed customers with questions to check them out as a first step toward finding answers.

PMI reaps rewards beyond the customer service function. When numbers of people began talking about a product on the Web site, they became a cohesive and loyal community. When the company has a problem with, say, quality control, these folks are the first to be supportive. They also share

their ideas for new or improved product lines—and alert
the company when a new product fails to measure up. That

happened with PMI's ATB mixer,
which started out with four
auxiliary send channels. The forum
members protested that more
were needed, and the company
responded by redesigning the
product to include six channels
instead of four.

In 2006, a hacker wreaked havoc with PMI'S forums, and
Alan Hyatt had to shut them down and start all over again,
rebuilding from scratch. No fun. The strength of the Internet
is its openness and lack of restraints, but those very strengths
leave online communities prey to Internet predators. They
are an infinitesimal minority of the online crowd, but as in so
many areas of life, one rotten apple can do a lot of damage.

Intuit

When this financial software powerhouse set up shop in
1984, its first product was Quicken, which has now been
purchased by more people than all other personal finance
software items combined. Two decades later, Quicken's
parent company, Intuit, decided to test the idea of customer-
support forums, but it wanted to avoid the hassles of building
and managing them. So it turned to LiveWorld, a specialist
in creating, operating, and moderating social networks and
online communities.

The Quicken forums are organized according to products
and computer type, PC or Mac. Other customers quickly
answer Quicken queries, usually in helpful detail. In fact,
the company says that volunteers answer 70 percent of all
support questions, taking an enormous load off customer

WHAT YOU CAN DO

❖ **Rate the experts.** When the product is complex, as is the case with PMI, the demands on customer forum personnel are greater—and so is the need to maintain constant surveillance. The surest way is to ask visitors to the site to rate the solutions they receive. Forum volunteers who consistently earn low scores should be replaced; as mentioned earlier, those who receive consistently high scores should be in line for rewards.

❖ **Bring in the pros.** By surveying questions and answers in the customer forums and in e-mails and calls to office staff, you should be able to spot problems that are causing customer experts the most difficulty. Organize occasional tutorials whereby the staff can provide the right answers to these and any other problems the volunteers are experiencing.

service employees. For example, when ten-year customer "Allan" complained that some of his mutual fund data wasn't showing in a Quicken capital gains report, several other customers began a dialogue. Some wrote lengthy explanations of the entire capital-gains process, and all offered the kind of caveats most employees would shun.

Of course, LiveWorld and its competitors charge for their services. Whether a company wants to take that route to get customers to serve themselves depends on its culture, finances, and technical savvy. But it's an option that a number of major companies, including America Online, Campbell Soup, Dove, and MINI Cooper, have embraced.

In the chapter just ahead, we examine what might seem to be the most unlikely of all crowdsourcing applications: the use of a customer community to sell products and services to its members and to consumers. Yet, as you will see, the logic behind the approach is unassailable. In fact, major corporations have begun to follow that route and are achieving major breakthroughs in sales and profits.

WHAT YOU CAN DO

❖ **Check your ego at the (virtual) door.**
Inevitably, forum volunteers will come up
against questions they can't
answer. Your job is to make
sure they quickly move the
question to higher authority,
whether by e-mail or by
phone. Volunteers need to
be drilled in the philosophy
that the ultimate goal is to
solve customer problems, and
individual egos should never
get in the way.

❖ **Talk straight.** "Allan," the Quicken
customer mentioned earlier, reaped one
of the major benefits of the online service
forums: the willingness
of the customer experts
to mention product
weaknesses. Of course,
none of your employee
experts is going to go on
record criticizing your
company's products. But as you know, what
counts above all if you want to keep his or
her business is that the customer be treated
well and fairly.

04

Customer, Sell Thyself

Yes, Procter & Gamble is in the business of turning out consumer products by the barrelful. As its Web site boasts, "Three billion times a day P&G brands touch the lives of people around the world." But the company has another, very different line of business as well. It offers up the services of hundreds of thousands of moms and teenagers as word-of-mouth marketers—for its own product divisions and those of other organizations as well.

Donna Wetherell, of Columbus, Ohio, is one of those "mom connectors," as they're called. She's employed at a customer service call center, where she's known as "the coupon lady." That's because she's always passing out P&G coupons and sharing news of new products with her 300 coworkers. They enjoy her visits, too.

"Dollars alone don't build a brand."

—ROBERT J. DAVIS

All of us like to chat about the goods we buy and use. Each week, the average person mentions specific brands 56 times in the course of 100 conversations. And studies have shown that today's consumers rely far more on what their friends and colleagues have to say about a product than on the ads they see on television. That's why, whether in person, on the phone, or online, the messages carried by Donna Wetherell and her connector colleagues are so often welcome. "We know," says Steve Knox, chief executive officer of Vocalpoint, "that the most powerful form of marketing is an advocacy message from a trusted friend."

P&G's word-of-mouth operation has two distinct pieces: Vocalpoint and Tremor. The Vocalpoint unit focuses primarily on P&G products and boasts 500,000 mothers who have children under 19. The Tremor unit focuses mainly on products from clients other than P&G and includes 250,000 teenagers. Proprietary research techniques enabled the company to find teens and moms who are gregarious and rich in friends. The average teenager has 25 friends on her instant message buddy list, while teen connectors have 150 or so. Mom connectors talk to 25 or so people a day, versus 5 for the average mother.

When P&G set about introducing its new dishwashing detergent, Dawn Direct Foam, it hired Vocalpoint to organize a crowdsourcing campaign. This is how Steve Knox describes what happened next: "Our connector moms looked at this product and went, 'Wow! That's so cool. My kids would want to help.'" That reaction led Knox to establish the talking points for his word-of-mouth army. In discussions with friends and colleagues, they would offer some "helpful hints" on how to get kids to do more chores around the house.

After that, Knox explains, "Dawn became a natural part of the conversation." The results: "We nearly doubled Dawn's business in the test market."

In 2005 the milk industry was preparing a national campaign to convince teenagers to forego sodas and drink milk as a way to reduce weight and body fat. Tremor's piece of it was to use word-of-mouth marketing to get teens who were drinking one glass of milk a day to drink more.

Teen connectors were sent a mailer that listed the benefits of drinking three glasses of milk a day ("achieve the look you want") and white "3X/day" bracelets to share with friends. In phone and e-mail messages, the connectors urged people to sign up for the 3X Challenge, offering them a chance to download a diary to keep track of their progress. Those who did received a cup and a bracelet by mail. The results: In no time, the effort had 1.5 million teenagers talking about milk. And according to

Tom Nagle, senior vice president of the International Dairy Food Association, "We were able to measure big increases in consumption in test versus control markets."

What started at P&G as a means to better peddle its own products has now become a profit center with clients ranging from cereal maker Kashi to cable channel Animal Planet to lubricant manufacturer WD-40. "We know," says Knox, "that the most powerful form of marketing is an advocacy message from a trusted friend." Or as P&G's CEO A. G. Lafley likes to say, "The consumer has become the marketer."

"Next to doing the right thing, the most important thing is to let people know you are doing the right thing."

—JOHN D. ROCKEFELLER

Procter & Gamble's success with word-of-mouth sales is just one example—although an impressive one—of the role this revolutionary breed of crowdsourcing can play in a marketing program. We use *revolutionary* advisedly. After all, merchants have relied on their customers to "spread the word" about their goods at least since the earliest Egyptians bartered their grain for olive oil or honey in the markets of Memphis. It's just that mobilizing huge numbers of people to take on that task, and paying them nothing or next to nothing to do so, puts a whole new, directed spin on an old, spontaneous practice.

By far the majority of P&G's connectors are upbeat about its products, but, of course, there are no controls on what they actually say. Some comfort can be found in studies that show that when Americans talk about brands, positive mentions outnumber negative by 6 to 1.

In the balance of this chapter, we offer more examples of the community as salesperson, along with some suggestions for how you can put all those people to work in your behalf.

M80

Back in 1998, Dave Neupert had an idea he thought would eventually be heard loud and clear in the marketing world. That's why he called his new company M80 Interactive Marketing, after the big-bang daddy of all firecrackers.

The story opens two years earlier, when Neupert was working at a record company in Los Angeles and eager to promote his clients through the Internet. He began setting up Web sites for bands, including one for the Deftones. It was the company's first with a chat room, and Neupert soon realized that a community of enthusiastic fans was forming around the site. Many of them complained that the band's music wasn't being played much on the radio. Neupert suggested they mobilize, using the Internet to spread the word. They did, and in short order, Deftones record sales started to rise.

Neupert got the message—and founded M80. Then, as now, the company followed a basic three-step formula:

1. Find rabid fans of the band, TV show, or whatever product he was promoting.

2. Convince them to push the product online, pretty much gratis.

3. Teach them how to go about it.

The fans he pursued were primarily young, and the products he asked them to push were those that had some cult popularity among the young. In an early interview, he described the crowdsourcing  campaign he ran in 1999 to promote a new album for the band *NSYNC. The volunteer online crew consisted of 4,000 people, mainly teenage girls. "We build huge blitz teams, as we like to call them," he says. They were urged to go onto Web sites where music fans congregated, including those of radio stations, to spread the word that a new *NSYNC album was due to hit the street shortly. "These fans are competitive in the boy-band community," according to Neupert. "They wanted to beat the Backstreet Boys' first-week sales record. We spread that word to fans that we had to beat that record."

A WORD FROM WE

"With communication costs decreasing,
feedback has become significantly more
cost effective. Hundreds of thousands
of discussion groups, rating systems,
e-mail threads, and blogs offer completely
unsolicited complaints, comments, and advice
for every product known to man."

—DONNA PITTERI, MEMBER OF THE WE ARE
SMARTER COMMUNITY

Then and now, M80 feeds its teams "inside" information
about client tours or videos and the date an ad campaign
is due to kick off. Knowing when radio stations are going
to carry promotions for a band, for
example, can spur a team to greater
efforts. "We tell them, 'Let's drive
the spins up,'" he says. Core team
members are rewarded with T-shirts,
tickets, and other items.

Since the early days, the company has
spread its wings. It has helped some
150 clients including many outside
the music industry, such as Comedy
Central, The Gap, Tommy Hilfiger, Honda, Napa Auto Parts,
Cingular Wireless, and Fox Broadcasting. Revenues rose to $2
million a year.

Whether Neupert will be able to take his
technique into the realms of less exotic
products—toilet paper leaps to mind—
remains to be seen. He's optimistic.
"Everyone is passionate about something,"
he told the *Los Angeles Times*. "But we
need to harness that enthusiasm."

Meanwhile, he's not lacking for admirers in the marketing
world. In 2006, WPP Group, the giant marketing and
communications firm, acquired 51 percent of M80's stock. No
price was announced, but the sale demonstrated conclusively
that the leveraging of the online community for product sales
had come of age.

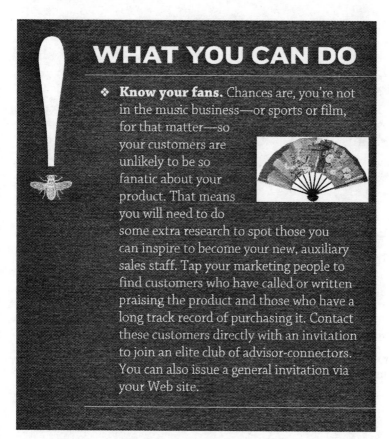

WHAT YOU CAN DO

❖ **Know your fans.** Chances are, you're not
in the music business—or sports or film,
for that matter—so
your customers are
unlikely to be so
fanatic about your
product. That means
you will need to do
some extra research to spot those you
can inspire to become your new, auxiliary
sales staff. Tap your marketing people to
find customers who have called or written
praising the product and those who have a
long track record of purchasing it. Contact
these customers directly with an invitation
to join an elite club of advisor-connectors.
You can also issue a general invitation via
your Web site.

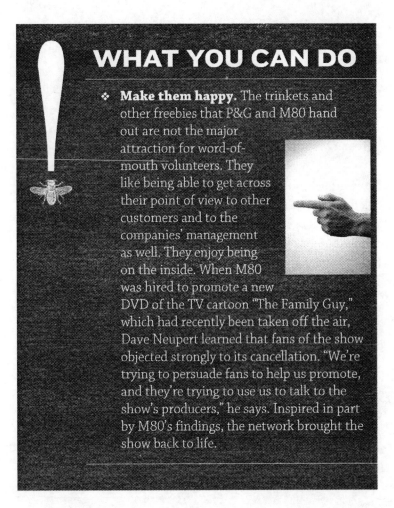

WHAT YOU CAN DO

* **Make them happy.** The trinkets and other freebies that P&G and M80 hand out are not the major attraction for word-of-mouth volunteers. They like being able to get across their point of view to other customers and to the companies' management as well. They enjoy being on the inside. When M80 was hired to promote a new DVD of the TV cartoon "The Family Guy," which had recently been taken off the air, Dave Neupert learned that fans of the show objected strongly to its cancellation. "We're trying to persuade fans to help us promote, and they're trying to use us to talk to the show's producers," he says. Inspired in part by M80's findings, the network brought the show back to life.

MasterCard

The advertising side of marketing has also tapped the online community for help in selling services and products. A pioneer in that regard was MasterCard, which invited visitors to its Web site to create their own versions of the highly successful "priceless" ads. Winners have been aired on television and posted on the www.priceless.com site, where visitors

are urged to vote for their favorites. Although no cash prizes were offered, the contest drew more than 100,000 entries.

A recent incarnation of the priceless promotion was a contest for college students, inviting them to write an essay and create a video about some aspect of their hometown that would make people want to visit. The winner was to spend the summer traveling around the world visiting some of these "priceless" places.

According to Joyce King Thomas, chief creative officer of MasterCard's advertising agency, McCann Erickson, "The campaign was interactive from the beginning. People wrote their own posters, made their own films, and did parodies."

Thomas and MasterCard could not have been thrilled by the parodies, thousands of which flooded Web sites; many of them were profane or obscene. "You're tapping into that consumer desire to have a piece of it," says Lawrence Flanagan, executive vice president and chief marketing officer at MasterCard worldwide. "You have to take the good with the bad."

#%@*!!!

In another contest tapping the online community, this time sponsored by USA Network, visitors to the company Web site were urged to upload videos of themselves as potential characters on USA Network shows; the winner appeared in a commercial and in an online series. The goal, according to Chris McCumber, a marketing vice president, was to allow members of the network's community to be "a part of the brand."

WHAT YOU CAN DO

❖ **Tap the talent.** Any sizeable community has large numbers of talented people—writers, artists, photographers—who are eager to see their work on display. When they invited their communities to create and upload videos, MasterCard and USA Network were well aware that a substantial number of the entries would be of little quality and less value. But they wanted to get these contestants to help in the process of binding customers and potential customers to their products and organizations. And they succeeded.

❖ **Narrow the target.** To reduce the number of off-subject and off-color videos uploaded, Yahoo! reached out to customers of a particular brand rather than the whole world of its Web site. Yahoo! Music urged fans of Shakira to turn out their own version of her video "Hips Don't Lie" and avoided the "priceless" problem. "I call it participation marketing," says Cammie Dunaway, chief marketing officer for Yahoo!. "Allow them to help you shape the brand experience."

> "Never write an advertisement which
> you wouldn't want your family to read.
> You wouldn't tell lies to your own wife.
> Don't tell them to mine."

—DAVID OGILVY, LEGENDARY ADMAN

Circuit City, Overstock.com, Macy's, Sears, and More

The list of companies that have opened their Web pages to customer product reviews grows daily—and, on the face of it, that's pretty strange. Question: Since when have business leaders been willing to countenance, much less sponsor, the appearance of negative as well as positive comments about their products in public? Answer: Since they began to recognize that their customers wanted to speak their minds about products they care about. And since they learned that authentic customer reviews lure serious spenders to their sites and increase sales.

One 2006 study found that 77 percent of Internet shoppers depended upon customer reviews, and half described the reviews as "critical" to their purchases. In other words, members of the communities of customers at these stores are telling other customers which products to buy, and the other customers are buying them—a prime instance of crowdsourcing as marketing tool.

Along with the proliferation of customer product reviews on merchant Web sites has come a variety of independent third-party sites that offer the same service. Each provides a somewhat different spin.

Reevoo.com, for example, works directly with some of Great Britain's largest online retailers, such as Dixons and Jessops. It contacts people who have made a purchase at one of those sites and asks them to give the item a mark from 1 to 10 in assorted categories of interest.

One of the charms of the Reevoo site is that reviews on quality, ease of use, and the like are shown as they are written by the customer so the visitor gets all sorts of down-to-earth, practical comments—"The screen scratches very easily," for example, or "The camera is a silly shape to have swinging round your neck."

When we visited the site, we found that Colin of Newcastle Upon Tyne had given his new Samsung HDTV-ready, LCD model a 9 (as did seven out of eight others surveyed, by the way), saying the picture and sound quality were "excellent." However, "by the time the TV [was] fully set up," Colin warned, the "stand had become rocky even when [the] fittings [were] re-tightened." Besides Colin's Samsung report, more than 300 other television reviews were listed, covering 38 brands.

Clicking on "Vacuum Cleaners" brought up 116 reviews of 20 brands, including one by David from Glasgow, who wasn't all that thrilled with the Bosch model he had chosen. David gave it a 3, citing a "poorly designed bagless dust box" that "clogs up very quickly (a sweet wrapper can foul it 100 percent)." He went on to say that the thing was "difficult to empty, and the plastic tags have broken already."

Other Bosch models ranked much higher with those who volunteered their opinions.

Reevoo emphasizes that, unlike product reviews on other sites, such as Amazon, its system virtually weeds out spam and overly flattering comments from the manufacturer disguised as unbiased customer comments. The company never pays its reviewers, on the theory that when money changes hands, bias can sneak in and compromise the quality of the appraisal.

Reevoo, which was founded in 2004, collects a fee from its partner retailers for being able to display the ReevooMark on their Web sites. As of spring 2007, the company had carried 60 million reviews and ratings.

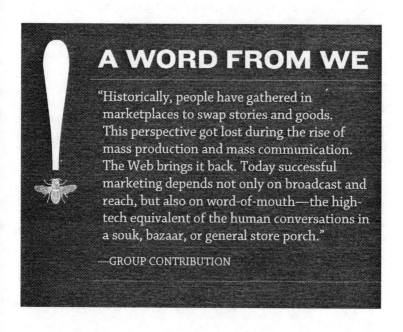

A WORD FROM WE

"Historically, people have gathered in marketplaces to swap stories and goods. This perspective got lost during the rise of mass production and mass communication. The Web brings it back. Today successful marketing depends not only on broadcast and reach, but also on word-of-mouth—the high-tech equivalent of the human conversations in a souk, bazaar, or general store porch."

—GROUP CONTRIBUTION

Angieslist.com, based in Indianapolis, charges its 500,000 members $10 to join and $6 a month for the privilege of

reading other members' reviews of local service businesses, from plumbers and electricians to nail parlors and dogwalkers. It has chapters in more than 100 cities.

Other privileges of Angie's List membership include a local monthly magazine (which evolved from a newsletter), discounts at some companies, and a call-in service to help find the right provider in an emergency, such as with a broken water pipe. On the basis of their individual experience, members rate a service provider from A to F on such factors as price, quality, punctuality, and responsiveness. They also fill out reports describing the particular job, which can be most revealing. One comment by a member who hired someone to prepare a home for sale, including painting, plaster work, and new flooring: "What was to be a 3- to 5-day job turned into a 37-day nightmare."

The founder of the site, Angie Hicks, has spent more than a decade organizing what she calls a homeowners' grapevine online. When members are looking for, say, a roofer, they can click on that category for a list of local roofers that have been rated, along with such data as their current grade and whether they offer any Angie's List discounts. Clicking on the individual company name opens a full profile.

WHAT YOU CAN DO

❖ **Honesty pays.** Enticing your online community to write customer reviews of your products can deliver a powerful marketing tool, but it can quickly turn sour if customers suspect you've planted all those positive reviews. Overstock.com had that sort of problem: Customer reviewers wanted to know why their upbeat comments were showing

up on the site, but not their negative ones. It turned out that the critical comments were being deep-sixed by managers in charge of the under-the-gun product lines. (Incidentally, Overstock leveraged its review system by stocking up on and promoting items that got very high ratings.) If you open your site to customer reviewers, you have to be willing to take the negative with the positive—that's the trade-off for gaining the trust and loyalty of your customers.

WHAT YOU CAN DO

❖ **Make your (multiple) choice.** If you want to include customer reviews in your company's operations, you can go in two basic directions: Hire an outsider or go it alone. Using an outsider risks losing control of the process, so you would have to set up mechanisms within your company to closely supervise your supplier. Going it alone requires that you have employees assigned to your Web site who can be counted on to monitor comments for irrelevant or objectionable content while making sure not to lose negative reviews. The success of a review page rests in part on the clarity and completeness of the introduction and explanations. In that regard, we tilt toward getting best-practice advice from outside experts.

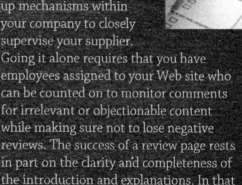

The growth and public popularity of customer reviews and the other examples of crowdsource marketing speak directly to a basic change in the nature of the relationship between you and your customer. The old commercial model in which you presented the products for sale and the customer simply chose among them is fast eroding. Today the customer is increasingly calling the shots. She's telling the world whether she likes or hates particular products she's tried. If you invite her, she's also up for making a few suggestions on how you might improve a product. Tomorrow she will insist on your coming up with new products that precisely meet her taste, telling you how they should be marketed and distributed, and proclaiming how well you've handled those tasks.

You can try to hold back the tide, maintaining your old way of doing business. You can find out what the customer wants and provide it. Or, best of all, you can determine where she's headed and get there ahead of her.

In the next chapter, we explore another area in which the community is altering traditional business patterns: manufacturing. In company after company, the crowd is actually producing the organization's product—and doing a great job of it.

05

If We Build It, We Will Come

There was a time—just a few years ago, really—when
thousands of highly skilled, professional photographers
counted on the licensing of their work by stock photo houses
to pay a big chunk of their rent. Not anymore. A lethal
combination of new technology and crowdsourcing is doing
them in.

This is the way it used to work: To illustrate their wares,
magazines, ad agencies, corporate publications, and film
companies routinely turned to photo agencies that stored
collections of shots by professionals. Customers might have
to pay fees of $100 or more for the one-time use of a photo,
but that was still a lot cheaper than assigning a photographer
to do the job. As magazine circulations declined and ad
budgets were cut, the fees fell, too, but they still provided a
safety net for the pros in an increasingly unstable business.

Enter the digital camera. Suddenly, anyone
with a semblance of skill was able to produce
accurate, attractive images. If the first shot
didn't work, you could always keep trying
until it did. And when you learned how to use

"Snowflakes are a fragile thing, but look at what they can do when they stick together."

—FERNANDO BONAVENTURA

Photoshop, you could make your image even better. If you had enough friends with digital cameras, you didn't need to hire a professional photographer to record your wedding, birthday, or family reunion.

Enter crowdsourcing. With all those millions of people clicking away on their digital cameras, millions of images were sitting around on computers.  Most of the photos weren't professional quality, but there were an awful lot of good shots just taking up space. So it wasn't long before microstock houses, as they're known, began to appear on the Internet to tap that huge supply of digital images. The newcomers charged customers as little as $1 for a royalty-free license.

The pioneer was Calgary-based iStockphoto, which giant Getty Images bought in 2006 for $50 million. The iStock library holds more than 1.7 million images from 36,000  members, and it has been blessed with Getty's advanced search and index technology, which makes it much easier for customers around the world to find just what they're looking for. The photos might not be up to the quality you'll find at Getty Images itself, but they have been selected by the company's editors, so they're apt to be just fine if you're putting together an office newsletter or even a magazine spread. And the price will be right.

iStock introduced a payment system that has become the industry standard. The minimum purchase is $12, which gives you 10 credits; images cost between 1 and 15 credits per download. The prices rise with the image size and resolution. iStock photos are downloaded at the rate of one every 2.5 seconds.

One reason for the site's success has been its welcoming content from contributors. The images are accompanied by symbols indicating how many of their photos have been sold through iStock and whether the work has been chosen for special attention on the site. Articles on the site offer photographic and design advice, and forums enable contributors to exchange news and speak their minds. The royalties many receive are impressive— exclusive contributors earn, on average, $1,000 a month. Also, they're happy about having other people see their work.

In this chapter, our focus is on the role of communities in manufacturing companies' products or, as in the case of iStock, content. The advantages over traditional business models are huge. At iStock, for instance, contributors not only create the product being sold, but they also deliver it in a market-ready format and list it in the appropriate keyword category. With little or no product inventory expense or traditional overhead, the company can price the product far below that of old-model competitors.

Here are some more examples
of crowdsourcing at work
providing companies with
their content. We hope the
variety will suggest how close
to infinite are its potential
applications—within your
company or any company you
might choose to create. And
take note: We haven't even
included Wikipedia.

Zebo.com

Joanna Z's fondest hopes and dreams, she tells her friends
on Zebo.com, include owning a pair of thousand-dollar
Lanvin pumps. When she sees something else she covets, she
drools—and types, "Look at that conical black heel. Sigh."

Zebo, one of a growing number of so-called social shopping
sites, is home to more than five million young and some not-
so-young materialists. They travel from one member's page to
another, taking in each other's photographs, profiles, blogs,
and lists of products desired and products possessed. By and
large, they are not searching out people for their character
traits or even their looks; it's their belongings that count. And

if by chance all that window-
shopping brings on a buying
urge, it can be satisfied at
ZeboShops, an e-commerce
page just a click away.

Launched in 2006 by Roy de Souza, a veteran marketing strategist, Zebo bills itself as "the world's largest repository of what people own." It reflects de Souza's conviction that young people today are what they own. "They list things because it defines them," he says.

Most members range between the ages of 16 and 25, although there are kids as young as 13 and some five times

that age. Take "Sircharlie M, 63, divorced," who says he owns a house, a 2004 Chevy truck, and eight remote-controlled aircraft that he built himself. Now Sircharlie is hoping to find "a nice lady to date."

There are all sorts of other things to find. Under "Celebrity Profiles," you can see "what the stars own and want, as reported by them!"

Mike James, for one, a point guard who in 2007 signed a four-year, $23-million contract with the NBA's Minnesota Timberwolves, listed a plasma television, a Playstation, soul food, Mexican food, chicken noodle soup, two pit bulls, tattoos, a Lincoln Navigator, and a Maserati among his possessions. His wish list includes "lots of video games," a Nissan Quest, and a Ford F-250 truck.

At the ZEBuzz forum, you can have real-time conversations "with other people who are bored, too!" You can start a group of your own about anything you want.

Product information of sorts can be found on ZE'Answers, where members pose and respond to shopping- and product-related questions. One day, Taylor asked about the most popular cell phone color. Eighty-six people replied to Taylor, including one who didn't actually own a cell phone but offered this comment: "Who cares what color it is, as long as it works good? A nonworking phone isn't worth having."

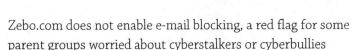

Zebo.com does not enable e-mail blocking, a red flag for some parent groups worried about cyberstalkers or cyberbullies pursuing young members. Other critics say that boasting online about owning expensive cars, audio and visual equipment, jewelry, and the like is like giving a burglar your house keys and leaving the light on for him.

But it seems more likely that Zebo members will become the targets of marketers rather than burglars. Regular visitors to the site willingly provide reams of information about their product preferences and buying habits, marketable data that is easily accessible to everyone. That has not escaped the notice of de Souza, who is also the CEO and cofounder of Zedo Inc., a Silicon Valley Internet ad serving business.

Under the heading "See New Stuff," which pitches "cool new products from many stores," members and visitors are linked to thousands of items that they are encouraged to rate, blog about, add to their wish lists, or buy outright. A foray into this section turned up everything from a $3 "Scotty Greeting Card from Coi" to a $425 ruby. Clicking on a picture of a product brings up a rating bar and the question "Is this [item] in or out?" The viewer then has the option of ranking the item on a scale of 1 to 10.

There are unofficial merchants as well. Brenda, a self-identified 52-year-old divorcee, lists 19 items she owns and lusts for more, particularly from French fashion designer Louis Vuitton. But if you scroll down to "Brenda's Zebo blog," you discover that she is, in fact, a reseller of trendy designer merchandise, "straight from the factory floor," which she's selling for "even less than wholesale!!!!!" Her business Web sites and a phone number are provided.

Whatever you may think of connecting people via their materialistic yearnings, you have to admit that de Souza has found an ingenious means of getting a huge community of mainly young people to supply him with content that draws ever more of them to his site. That's what crowdsourcing is all about.

ThisNext.com

As with Zebo, ThisNext relies on members to create its content—namely, lists of their favorite products. Also, like Zebo, ThisNext provides links to stores.

WHAT YOU CAN DO

❖ **Get emotional.** What makes Zebo.com and so many other community-driven sites successful is its basic premise: Young people are passionate about possessions, those they own and those they want. That's an important message for anyone thinking about using crowdsourcing as a manufacturing process. The crowd will not come to you unless you touch them where they live. No one wants to devote time and dollars to a site about your new brand of aspirin; a site dedicated to exchanging news and views about pain control is more likely to succeed.

❖ **Get the crowd involved.** As the Zebo site suggests, the more ways you can provide visitors with a chance to express themselves, the more likely they will hang around and identify with your operation. Forums, targeted question-and-answer pages, ratings systems—they're all calculated to keep members busy and involved and eager to keep delivering up more content. It's a virtuous circle.

When you enter the name of an item in the search bar, you end up on pages with a variety of nominations and links to the nominators. We typed in "surfboard," for example, and discovered 22 options, from miniature surfboard towel hooks ("They brighten up a kid's bathroom," wrote Jody) to a Rusty shortboard ("Thin as a chip, turny but definitely not a flip flopper,"

according to Allyson). In each case, we were informed how many members recommended an item and what tags were applicable to the choice ("waves," "Venice"). We were also told where the item could be purchased.

ThisNext, once again like Zebo, is known as a social shopping site. It enables its members to create their own pages with a photo, a profile, and answers to a long series of questions, such as "What is the next big step you'd like to make?" It also allows them to go to other members' blogs to find more examples of their product tastes or simply to establish contact. And although the member lists on ThisNext are weighted toward products, they can range far and wide, from activities (cooking and climbing, for example) to entertainment (movie reviews), to lifestyles (living green).

In theory, everyone posting products is a private citizen, but it's easy for a company's employees to sign up as individuals and promote the company's product. Some consultants actually advise clients to do so as a means of "building buzz" around a product. Still, such recommendations are in the minority. As a member told the *New York Times*, "I like the concept of peers, people like me, referring each other to interesting things. It's more trustworthy."

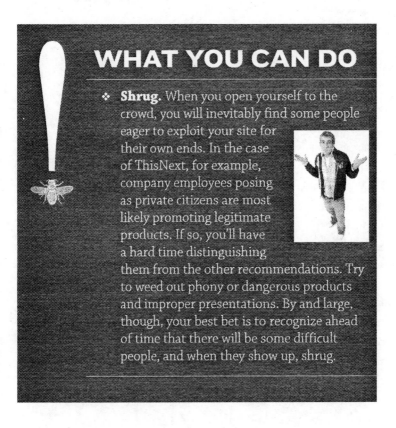

WHAT YOU CAN DO

* **Shrug.** When you open yourself to the crowd, you will inevitably find some people eager to exploit your site for their own ends. In the case of ThisNext, for example, company employees posing as private citizens are most likely promoting legitimate products. If so, you'll have a hard time distinguishing them from the other recommendations. Try to weed out phony or dangerous products and improper presentations. By and large, though, your best bet is to recognize ahead of time that there will be some difficult people, and when they show up, shrug.

VirtualTourist.com

This site, which first appeared in 1999, boasts more than 880,000 registered members and 5 million unique visitors a month. The founders, convinced that the most valuable travel advice comes from other travelers, envisioned a wikinomics-style site where people could share their travel experiences and photographs, and offer tips about local hotels, restaurants, and attractions. That's happened, all right: 1.48 million travel tips on more than 27,000 locations, 2.9 million photos. Forums enable visitors to ask members questions, 85 percent of which are answered. But members have greatly expanded the nature of the site, sharing information about themselves and making friends. Beyond that, many members have moved VirtualTourist out of the virtual world. They are meeting offline, contributing new content there that eventually finds its way back to the site.

The home page presents a list of so-called travel guides, made up of members' contributions. Each guide is organized under 13 main headings, including "Local Customs" and "Tourist Traps." In Bangkok, along with ads and sponsored links, we found connections to a forum about the city and to discounts on hotels and the like. There was also a list of members, including a Bangkok resident, who had written about the city. Members are encouraged to e-mail contributors for more information.

One of the members who had weighed in on Bangkok—SirRichard, by name—actually lived in Madrid. (His motto: "When in doubt, move.") But he had visited and filed descriptions of 47 countries, ranging from *A* (Albania) to *Z* (Zimbabwe). The general descriptions of his visits might have come from a travel book, but his tips were detailed,  personal, and, from the vantage point of other Bangkok visitors, right on target. SirRichard was ranked the fifth most popular contributor on the site, based on the ratings his tips had received from other members.

Fed up with glossy travel publications that too often view destinations through rose-tinted glasses, millions of people

now tap into VirtualTourist, and dozens of major companies—
from American Airlines to Westin Hotels—are happy to place
ads in a virtual environment that deals in realities.

WHAT YOU CAN DO

❖ **Vary content.** It seems obvious now:
1. The public wants honest, dependable
information about travel. 2.
Travelers love to share their
experiences. VirtualTourist
simply combined those two
facts and created a popular
and potentially profitable
site. The same equation can work for you,
whether you're hoping to crowdsource
content for an existing company or for a
new company of your own creation. Find
something the public wants and needs;
present it in such a way that an enthusiastic
community will form to meet that demand.

❖ **Vary venues.** Although so much of today's
crowdsourcing occurs on the Internet, you
should be alert to other venues. The
offline meetings of VirtualTourist
members are a case in point.
Commercial opportunities abound
wherever a community exists around
an idea or an emotion. The Internet
is the most popular medium for marshalling
a crowd in your behalf, but it's not the
only one.

A WORD FROM WE

"So, outside inventors, outside thought leaders, outside designers to the extent that it makes sense. We believe that there are ideas out there that can benefit our company."

—MICHAEL PERMAN, LEVI STRAUSS

ChaCha.com

Even as you read this, somewhere in or above the United States, maybe in a nearby house or the next seat on the plane, a figure sits hunched over a computer, ready and willing to answer any question you might have about anything at any time of the day or night. That's the premise, and the promise, of ChaCha.com, which was founded in December 2005 in Carmel, Indiana, by two impatient entrepreneurs.

ChaCha's chairman and CEO, Scott Jones, invented, at the age of 25, the world's most popular voice mail system (now used by more than 1 billion subscribers). He went on to establish companies in fields as disparate as music-recognition technology and robotics. His innovations show up in Apple's iPod and in robotic lawnmowers. Brad Bostic, ChaCha president, founded Bostech Corporation, which has evolved from custom software development into an enterprise integration software provider; he also built NearMed, a telemedicine service for healthcare providers.

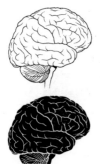 What the two men were impatient about, back in 2005, was traditional search engines. It was taking them too long to sort through the dozens or hundreds of irrelevant answers provided before finding one they were looking for. Their solution was a Web site that combined the investigative talents of machines and the human brain.

A ChaCha search starts when you enter a search term. The instant results are the combination of the best search technology and so-called hand picked sites from the ChaCha community of skilled search experts known as ChaCha guides. If you require further assistance, you can select the option to work directly with a guide. An instant message chat session will begin, and a guide will greet you with a typed message indicating that he or she is ready to help you with your search. Once a guide clarifies what you need, he or she will find the most relevant information and display only those links. If you're not satisfied with your guide's work, you can ask for another.

As of fall 2007, Scott Jones expects to have a community of about 50,000 guides at work, assisting in providing content, and 1 million users of the site. The guides are trained and generally paid between $5 to $10 a search hour—the rate depends upon the reviews they receive from those they help and the number of searches they conduct. The success of the enterprise, all parties agree, will depend on just how good the guides are.

ChaCha searches are free; the
founders hope to make their money
in part, at least, from on-site
advertising. Their serious income,
they say, will come when their
service becomes available to cell
phone users via a toll-free number.

Voice-recognition software will take care of simple searches
such as sport scores, and other searches will be turned over to
the guides. The founders predict that advertisers will be eager
to fill the 15 to 30 seconds when callers are on hold, awaiting
search results.

In case you were wondering, the company's name isn't a
reference to the cha-cha; rather, it comes from the Chinese
word *cha*, which means "search."

Current TV

Viewer-created content, or VC2, makes up about a third
of what's seen on this 24-hour, San Francisco–based,
independent cable and satellite channel—and, not so
incidentally, another non-Internet crowdsourcing venue. The
work makes its way to the television screen by way of a voting
system in which a community of viewers votes on whether
a five-minute piece of film is worthy to be shown on the
airwaves. But getting the green light from viewers still doesn't
guarantee air time; Current TV's producers have the final say
as to which of the viewer-chosen clips are ready for prime
time.

Started by former Vice President Al Gore and entrepreneur
fundraiser Joel Hyatt in August 2005, the channel had a
number of early detractors. *The Wall Street Journal* ridiculed
it, for example, as "newsless, often clueless, and usually dull

WHAT YOU CAN DO

❖ **Maintain quality.** As with many crowdsourced sites, ChaCha has taken steps to keep tabs on its content providers by encouraging customers to rate the guides. (Need we point out that this approach is yet another example of the all-pervasiveness of crowdsourcing? Customers are doing the work that employees handle in traditional organizations.) eBay, for example, has buyers rating sellers on everything from the speed of delivery to the condition of the item delivered. You have visitors to your site only as long as they're getting the kind of feedback they want, so anything that gets in the way—any failure in the quality of the operation—can easily send them searching elsewhere. Constant vigilance, by employees and/or customers, is the price of profit.

❖ **Go medium rare.** So much of crowdsourcing in this book and elsewhere is mediated by the Internet, which is, in fact, the proximate cause of the whole phenomenon, that ChaCha's telephonic twist is welcome news. The simplicity of the notion is also attractive: No need to fire up the computer or type in search words—just type a few words into the receiver, and your questions get answered. It's as though some Iron Age tool turned out to be a neat substitute for an electronic gadget. The serious message is, look upon every kind of community, on- and offline, as a potential crowdsourcing partner.

... a limp noodle." Based on what's happened in the intervening two years, it turns out that the *Journal* was the clueless one, seriously underestimating the power of wikinomics. Short videos made by up-and-coming filmmakers, citizen reporters, and the viewers themselves are constantly grabbing headlines, and sites such as YouTube, Google Video, and Yahoo! have shown just how popular audience-created entertainment can be.

And Current TV has a couple of very important advantages over these other sites. For one, it has a leg up in ad production. Companies such as Sony, L'Oreal, and Toyota show commercials made by Current TV viewers, and that typically means a member of the much-sought-after 18-to-34 demographic. So besides getting cut-rate deals on great commercials— L'Oreal paid $1,000 for a stunning and sophisticated viewer-created ad that would have cost it 150 times as much if produced in-house—the advertisers gain insight into the changing tastes of younger consumers.

Second—and, in the long run, maybe even more important— is the distinction between having one's video appear on a Web site and having your work shown on a bona fide television channel. Put another way, it's the difference between a dot-com company and all the baggage that term still carries, and a long-proven business model.

The pieces that make it onto Current TV are a varied palette of trendy cultural items and advocacy journalism that highlights issues such as the ongoing turmoil in the Middle East, poverty in Third World countries, the scourge of AIDs in Africa, and the devastation wrought by Hurricane Katrina. The Katrina piece, shot by a New Orleans resident, aired before network news reporters could even make their way to the city.

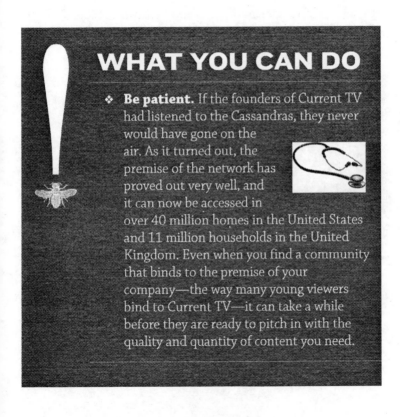

WHAT YOU CAN DO

❖ **Be patient.** If the founders of Current TV had listened to the Cassandras, they never would have gone on the air. As it turned out, the premise of the network has proved out very well, and it can now be accessed in over 40 million homes in the United States and 11 million households in the United Kingdom. Even when you find a community that binds to the premise of your company—the way many young viewers bind to Current TV—it can take a while before they are ready to pitch in with the quality and quantity of content you need.

The essential element that unites all the businesses in this chapter is the willingness—indeed, the eagerness—of the community involved to create product. Year after year, we see improvements in the technology that allows the crowd to produce content. Year after year, we see new online entries that take advantage of the power of community. The opportunities are virtually infinite, limited only by desire and imagination.

In the next chapter, we explore another of crowdsourcing's amazing contributions. Suddenly, there are sites that provide financing for business ventures that might otherwise never get off the ground. Need a loan? Have an idea for a way to tap into the huge cash resources of the crowd? The next chapter is for you.

06

Welcome to the World Bank of We

When Buddy, her cuddly Bichon Frise, hurt his paw, Lyn Townshend of Longmont, Colorado, refused to accept the so-called Elizabethan collar, the uncomfortable plastic cone that makes a dog look as though its head is stuck in a lampshade. So she sewed an elastic strap onto a sock and put the sock on Buddy's paw and the strap around his body, effectively covering the wound and keeping the dog from licking and chewing the dressing. She called it a Strock, combining *strap* and *sock,* and it was a lot more comfortable for the dog—not to mention a lot less attention-getting and embarrassing for its owner.

In fact, it was such a success that Townshend decided she had the makings of a commercial venture. Early in 2006, she formed Best Buddy Pet Products and began turning out designer Strocks on her home sewing machine (www.thestrock.com or www.bestbuddypetproducts.com). The new version was waterproof, came in different sizes to accommodate cats and other noncanine pets, and used adjustable Velcro straps. On just her third sales call, Townshend won the

"The buck doesn't even
slow down here."

—ANONYMOUS

endorsement of a veterinary hospital that was part of a 600-strong chain. Suddenly, it looked as though she would have to be ready to produce Strocks by the hundreds—without receiving payment until she delivered the finished goods.

What Townshend needed was a loan. The problem was, she had no income, having quit her job at IBM; she had a record of credit card delinquencies; and she had never run a company. Not surprisingly, she was turned down by her local bank and by the Small Business Administration.

What to do? Wikinomics! Turning to Prosper.com, she joined the community's Business Owners Cooperative, made up of past and would-be borrowers. She posted her loan request on her page at Prosper and would-be lenders bid on it, until finally she was funded by a total of 77 people. On May 21, 2006, she landed a loan of $9,500 at 12.75 percent interest—considerably less than she would have had to pay on a credit card. She used it to buy office equipment, arrange for mass production at a nearby factory, and get her product trademarked.

Prosper is a leading example of the power of community as financier, but it is just the latest twist in the ancient practice of people-to-people lending. Seventeen hundred years ago, long before there were banks or an Internet, there were communities in China called *lun-hui* whose members helped each other borrow cash. For centuries in the Caribbean, Africa, Korea, and Vietnam, there have been local money pools. Members contribute a set amount each week and take turns picking up the total at the month's end. Known as *susu* in the Caribbean, *kaes* in Korea, and *hui* in Vietnam, these lending societies are common in immigrant communities across the United States. As it happens, that's exactly how Prosper.com came into being.

Back in 1983, Lyna Lam and her family escaped from Vietnam and settled in San Jose, California. They had no income, and all seven of them lived in a studio apartment. Then they joined their neighbors, pooling what money they could scrape together in a *hui*. They used it to buy a car and, eventually, start a landscaping business.

Meanwhile, Chris Larsen was graduating from San Francisco State University with a degree in accounting. After spending a few years working for Chevron, he earned an MBA at Stanford and, in 1992, started a mortgage business. Four years later, he launched E-Loan, which closed more than $27 billion in consumer loans before he sold it to Popular Inc. in 2005 for $300 million. For his next act, Larsen established Prosper.com.

Where did he get the idea? Partially from his wife, Lyna Lam. As she told *Business Week,* "He was fascinated by how [the Vietnamese] work together and come through for each other."

The basic advantages of borrowing and lending on these sites are clear and simple: Borrowers pay less interest than they would otherwise; lenders get better returns.

Prosper came online in February 2006. It works very much like eBay, except that what is being auctioned is a loan, not a used bicycle or a collection of comic books. Registration is free. Borrowers get a page on the site to list the size of the loan they want—the upper limit is $25,000—and the interest rate they're willing to pay. They also present their reason for the loan and as much information about themselves as they think will help attract lenders. Prosper runs credit checks on potential borrowers, assigning them one of eight scores, from AA (the top rating) to HR ("High Risk"), to NC ("No Credit History"). It also provides the borrower's debt-to-income ratio. The auction can last from three to seven days, at the borrower's discretion.

Prosper encourages borrowers to join one of the thousands of groups that have formed around a single leader and generally consist of people who have something in common, whether service in the armed forces, or a degree from Penn State, or a divorce. By joining a group whose members have achieved a successful record of repaying loans, the borrower can attract more offers from lenders at lower rates because the group as a whole carries less risk of delinquency. The group leader provides guidance, but it can come at a price: The leader  can collect a reward of up to $20 when a member's loan gets funded—and another bonus each time a borrower makes a monthly payment on time. Many don't take these "shared rewards," though.

Because the groups function as separate communities within the larger community on the site, they exert a degree of discipline on their members. Like the members of a *hui*, group members fear losing face if they miss their payments. They are also aware that such behavior tarnishes the group's  record, with financial consequences for all its would-be borrowers.

Successful borrowers pay Prosper a 1 to 2 percent fee when a loan comes through, while registered lenders pay a 0.5 to 1 percent annual servicing fee on their outstanding loans. Just over a year after its founding, the company had marked up 11,100 loans totaling more than $65 million. Approximately 2 percent of funded loans in dollar terms or 3 percent (339 loans) of funded loans in unit terms have defaulted.

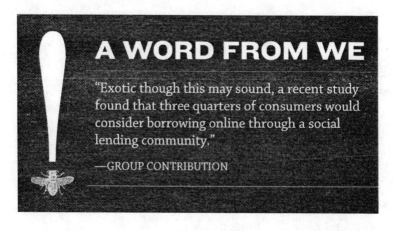

A WORD FROM WE

"Exotic though this may sound, a recent study found that three quarters of consumers would consider borrowing online through a social lending community."

—GROUP CONTRIBUTION

Zopa

Before there was Prosper.com, there was Zopa, established in spring 2005. Where Prosper presents itself in sober, bankerly fashion, Zopa has a chip on its shoulders toward banks and other stick-in-the-muds. "Whatever you call [us]," its Web site pleads, "please don't call us a bank." "Marketplace" is preferred. What's so bad about banks? They have "huge overheads, with thousands of employees to pay, hundreds of branches to *feng shui,* and countless fat cats to feed. And they take more than their fair share of people's money."

There are substantive differences as well between the two
social-lending sites, as they're known. Zopa does not rely on
separate communities of members to improve borrowers'
chances and diminish lenders' risks. Would-be borrowers
are put through credit checks and a risk-assessment process;
those who pass receive a rating from A* to C, depending on
their risk profile. Zopa offers borrowers a protection policy
that keeps those monthly repayment checks going in case of
illness, accident, or loss of job.

Lenders announce the rate of return they seek, what
level A* to C they want to lend to, and when
they want their money back. Their loans
are then divided into small chunks and
distributed among potential borrowers.
There must be at least 50 lenders for every
loan of 500 pounds or more, and no one is
allowed to borrow twice from the same person.
Lenders receive 4.5 percent interest on their funds
that have not yet been lent out.

As of the spring of 2007, *The Daily Telegraph* reported, Zopa
listed 135,000 members and an average annual return to
lenders of 6.8 percent. More than half of those applying for
Zopa loans flunk their credit checks and are turned down.
Something like 1 percent of A-rated borrowers are in default,
and that rises to 3 percent for C-rated borrowers.

In at least one department, Zopa is unashamed to compare
itself to banks: "A collections agency chases any missed
payments on each lender's behalf. This is exactly the same
process that banks and other financial institutions use." Of
course, unlike banks, Zopa's loans are not covered by Britain's
Financial Services Compensation Scheme—nor by America's
Federal Deposit Insurance Corporation, for that matter.

Yes, Zopa has launched itself into the
U.S. market with a base in San Francisco
and $15 million from Bessemer Venture
Partners, America's oldest venture
capital firm. "We can assure you, it will
be a distinctly American cake," the company promised, "more
of a brownie than a scone, if you like."

WHAT YOU CAN DO

❖ **Set the stage.** The initiators of a
crowdsourcing site or other venue need
to set a tone that will
feel welcoming to the
community they invite
in. Of course, it has to be
efficient, as both Prosper
and Zopa are, but it should
also have an appropriate personality.
Prosper, as you've seen, is the more proper,
bankerly site, while Zopa has something of
an edge and a greater sense of humor.

❖ **Go the extra mile.** It's almost as though
the creators of Zopa sat down, having put
the basic lending and borrowing procedures
in place, and said to
themselves, "What else can
we do to make members
feel comfortable?" And
they found things, too.
On the lenders' side, it was the decision to
pay decent interest on unlent loan money.
On the borrowers' side, it was the offering
of insurance against accident or job loss. It
only makes sense.

A WORD FROM WE

"Microlending Web sites provide the ability for individuals to lend to small businesses directly. The underwriting decisions (assessing the risk of each loan) are made by individuals, and the price of a loan is established through lender bidding. We expect these lending decisions to be superior to the same decisions currently made by experts at banks."

—REX MILLER, MEMBER OF THE WE ARE SMARTER COMMUNITY

CommonAngels

In June 1998, in a restaurant not far from the Boston Common, a handful of former software company CEOs sat down around a breakfast table and created something new in the world. As private investors, they had individually provided funds to support start-ups. They now agreed to become a community of angels, jointly considering, selecting, and financing high-potential, early-stage information technology companies. They decided to call their firm CommonAngels, in honor of those nearby historic meeting grounds.

Since then, this experiment in crowdsourcing has succeeded beyond its founders' dreams. Its membership has grown to 70 investors plus five dozen limited partners in two coinvestment funds. It has collectively funded 34 companies with $38 million and has had numerous successes. And it has inspired dozens of other groups of angel investors to follow suit.

In many ways, CommonAngels demonstrates the power inherent in community, not just in the finance area, but in every aspect of business. Because of the firm's communal nature, its members—seasoned entrepreneurs with expertise in software, IT, and the Internet—bring the sum of their knowledge and experience to every investment decision. They also bring their thousands of personal and professional relationships to bear, providing a strong flow of deals and relevant expertise. And because their own money is riding on it, they're seriously involved in the process.

An angel community is quite unlike a traditional venture capital (VC) operation. VC firms usually invest other people's money, based upon the judgment of managers who are paid a fee and a share of the profits, and face little or no downside risk. The members of the angel group win all or lose all. It makes for a very different decision-making process—and a very different investment profile.

According to James Geshwiler, a founder and a managing director of CommonAngels, a major benefit of the communal approach is that it can't be gamed. When a VC committee of three or four people sits down to vote on funding projects, each of the members is likely to have a favorite; to get his or her project approved by the others, a member will hedge his or her critique of their projects. The committee decisions also depend on the relationships among the members—who's up or down, who wants to impress whom. A clever start-up CEO can play to that audience.

"At CommonAngels, we get 40 people in a room," Geshwiler says. "That's too many to game. And they're all voting their own checkbook. So what do I care what you think about what I think? I only care about what you think about the company under consideration. I'm not going to hold back what I really think, and neither are you. We're going to draw each other out."

A start-up seeking support begins by e-mailing the angel group its business plan's executive summary. Geshwiler e-mails copies of the summary to a few members who are knowledgeable about the company's project area. If they're enthusiastic, the start-up's leader is invited to make a presentation to those members and another two or three

who are what Geshwiler calls "generalists." Specialists can become "victims of their own experience and make assumptions," he says. "Generalists ask the basic questions, such as 'Why is this such a good idea?'" Too often, he adds, an investor acting individually makes his or her decisions on the basis of only one or two risks, while failing to test more rigorously basic questions, such as: What are the fundamental dynamics of the market for the product? Or, how hard is it really to make the technology work? If the start-up passes muster at that level, its leader moves on to the final stage: a presentation before 40 or more members.

At every stage, the questions fly and the members discuss and debate the various issues with the start-up leader and with each other. Sometimes when an entrepreneur describes how he wants to build his company, Geshwiler says, "It's like watching the Red Sea part: the ex-Microsoft people on one side, the ex-Lotus people on the other, and a 20-year-old argument comes back—centralized architecture versus distributed systems."

Because of the checks and balances built into the community approach, CommonAngels reaches a consensus that is far more often right than wrong. But none of it is easy. Geshwiler offers an example of a start-up called Skyhook Wireless,

whose product, a virtual GPS, was capable of correcting the problem GPS has in big cities because the tall buildings block the line of sight to the satellite. The company said its invention could be used to fix GPS in automotive navigation systems, wi-fi cell phones, and other devices. The angel group "debated and debated" over which, if any, of the applications represented a substantial market, and finally decided to invest $1.5 million. Sure enough, the start-up has signed a major deal to have its product embedded in a GPS chip.

CommonAngels has developed techniques to avoid some
of the potential pitfalls of group decision making—the
bandwagon effect, for example, when members rush to join
an acknowledged expert after he offers an early review of
a company. After a presentation, the large group is divided
into separate tables of five or six people. Each table elects
a reporter who summarizes the table's conclusions for the
larger group. During the discussion, members are expected
to fill out and hand in so-called evaluation sheets indicating
their attitude toward the proposed investment. The goal is to
ensure that the members are exposed to all the arguments,
pro and con, and are given ample opportunity to make their
own feelings known.

The community's decisions, Geshwiler says, are based upon
assumptions about a company, including the abilities and
integrity of its leaders and the market for its products. After
an initial investment, CommonAngels insists on testing its
assumptions. It sends teams of members on follow-up visits
to the company, usually on a six-month schedule. Once again,
he explains, the numbers matter. When a VC firm's partner
who championed an investment in a company pays a follow-
up visit, that person is looking for good news because his
or her reputation in the firm is on the line. CommonAngels
members have no such concern. And with a whole team of
people, Geshwiler adds, the company's leader has far less
chance to hide his or her situation: "There's
a lot more incentive to just get
everything out on the table."
That comes in handy when
it's time to think about a
follow-up round of investing.

WHAT YOU CAN DO

❖ **Expertise is not everything.** As a community dedicated to making the right decision, CommonAngels recognized from the get-go that it needed a broad range of expertise in its chosen area of information technology. So it made sure its membership list included people with a wide variety of skills. At the same time, the firm brought in people whose entrepreneurial experience was outside technology—generalists who could look at a proposed deal from a larger, nontechnical perspective. Communities need both kinds of members.

❖ **Turn the discussion on its head.** From a sponsor's point of view, decision making in a community is fraught with potential problems—it's all too susceptible to all sorts of negative, ill-advised influences. A small group can easily lead the larger community down a path to a disastrous conclusion. A single charismatic individual can turn a discussion on its head. Personal agendas and personality conflicts can create havoc. What's needed are people, like CommonAngels' leaders, who have an understanding of group dynamics and can develop procedures to guard against such problems.

There's a wide divide between Prosper and Zopa, on the one hand, and CommonAngels, on the other—between Lyn Townshend's $9,500 loan to make Strocks and a million-dollar investment in a high-tech start-up. What we have tried to suggest is the close to infinite variety of ways in which communities can be used to perform a company's finance function. Approaches might vary, but in all cases, the focus is on finding ways to minimize the lender's risk by providing the maximum amount of relevant information.

The next chapter discusses the role crowdsourcing might play in actually managing an organization. Is such a thing possible? Turn the page, and you'll find out.

07

Make Everyone a C-We-O

Up to this point in the book, we have deluged you with successful examples of crowdsourcing at work—communities of individuals cheerfully performing virtually every business function, from product design to finance. This chapter is different because we have arrived at the activity that cuts across all functions: management. Here our central question is: Can a community successfully determine the direction of a company, making strategic decisions about what products or services to pursue and how to create, market, and distribute them?

The answer, to date, has been no—and not for lack of trying. Perhaps the most thorough and intensive effort so far was undertaken in June 2005 by Rob May, an engineer, an entrepreneur, and founder of Businesspundit.com. He established a project called TheBusinessExperiment.com (TBE), which quickly attracted more than 800 members, all of them eager to participate in what promised to be a historic, groundbreaking venture. Together members selected a product—another Web site—and it was eventually designed and launched. Sad to say, in March 2006, just nine months after its birth, TBE was voted out of existence.

"If things seem under control,
 you're not going fast enough."
—MARIO ANDRETTI

In a pointed essay on
Businesspundit.com, May
offered his explanation for the
failure of his experiment. "The
wisdom of crowds is huge right
now," he wrote. "Old businesses
are dead. It's all about

embracing edge competencies and network effects. ...
I don't buy it. Business is still business."

Yes, we agree, business is still business, but we beg to differ
with his other conclusions. There is simply too much evidence
of the successful leveraging of communities—successful in
traditional business terms—to write off the power of we. At
the same time, a number of vital lessons can be learned from
the short but fascinating TBE experience, particularly as it
pertains to the ability of a community to manage and lead an
organization.

The initial TBE Web site was envisioned as an incubator for a
fully transparent exercise in P2P, or peer-to-peer, creativity.
On it, visitors would become members; via discussion
forums, members would talk
about their plans, make decisions,
and read progress reports. Their
only reward, aside from personal
satisfaction in helping the site
move ahead, would be points based upon a member's
contributions to the project. Point totals would determine
what share of the hoped-for profits a member received.

During TBE's first weeks, members submitted some 60 ideas
for new businesses, which were debated in the forums and

then voted on in serial fashion. Finalists included a social-networking site for business travelers and a kiosk for selling MP3 files. In the end, members chose to create Askspace.com, which would tap the wisdom of members to provide solutions to problems small business owners presented.

Because members received equity, TBE had to file a private placement offering early on, and the legal costs were considerable. May had assumed that "someone with more money than sense" would "throw $25K" at the project, enabling it to pay legal bills and even outsource some of the technical work. It never happened. As a result, if Askspace was to succeed, the members would have to make it happen themselves.

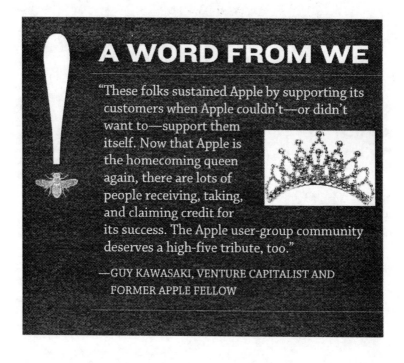

A WORD FROM WE

"These folks sustained Apple by supporting its customers when Apple couldn't—or didn't want to—support them itself. Now that Apple is the homecoming queen again, there are lots of people receiving, taking, and claiming credit for its success. The Apple user-group community deserves a high-five tribute, too."

—GUY KAWASAKI, VENTURE CAPITALIST AND FORMER APPLE FELLOW

When the final venture was settled
upon, though, many members lost
interest, presumably because the ideas
they favored had lost out. A third of
them never logged onto TBE again.
Only about 200 members remained
actively committed, and a mere 30 of
them joined four leadership teams. In
October, member David Gibbons wrote
on the site, "Organizing these groups
functionally has been a challenge,
mostly to the democracy that made TBE
so appealing in the first place."

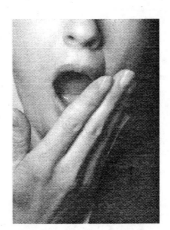

It had become evident that top-down leadership was needed,
and TBE member Sean Clauson, a database programmer
from Minneapolis, Minnesota, volunteered to become chief

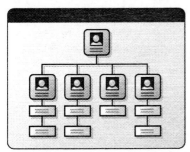

executive officer. As Rob
May put it, "Sean built a
leadership team and really
drove the project forward."
The five members of that
team met for the first time
in October, via Skype, and
talked for two hours.

High on their list of topics was the membership's remarkable
enthusiasm for Gibbons's proposal to split the new venture
into a large number of small tasks and allow members to
choose which they would take on, an approach known as
microchunking. More than 91 percent of the community
endorsed the plan, as compared to an average 41 percent
approval for the previous six proposals, including the
Askspace name.

As it turned out, though, members were better at voting than working. "We had an abundance of expert opinion," Gibbons wrote in March, "but those same experts' time is in very short supply, so getting actual work done became almost impossible." Nevertheless, a beta version of Askspace was launched.

Soon afterward, Rob May wrote, "We came to realize that the way we operated was no different from other companies. Decisions were made at high levels because there wasn't time to put everything up to a vote to the crowd. In addition, the crowd sometimes voted in ways that gave us conflicting direction." When he put Askspace's future to a vote, the nays won.

May offered several lessons TBE had taught him. For example, having members vote on which business idea to pursue was the wrong approach. He should have started with a new business clearly in mind. Then, he wrote, "I would have attracted the right people—people that liked that particular idea. Instead, I attracted people that primarily liked to discuss ideas."

To gain members' wholehearted support, May maintained, a P2P business must tailor its incentives to their tastes. TBE's members were "a successful bunch," he explained, and, as a consequence, they were short on time. Even 30 minutes a week turned out to be too much. What was needed was a truly involved and committed membership that would be satisfied by the intangible incentives of "knowledge, satisfaction of their curiosity, and the desire to succeed."

In the beginning, May had hoped the membership would be self-directed. He became convinced that this was an expectation not grounded in reality. Large groups, he wrote, need leaders who understand not only the whole project, but the context of all individual aspects of the project: "If everybody has an equal voice, it can lead to lots of talking in circles and very little productive decision making." At least, that's what happened at TBE.

Meanwhile, Askspace has an afterlife in the form of a site called Askspace.blogspot.com. It was established by Carolyn Burke, one of the first five leaders of TBE. (She is also generally accorded the honor of having invented the blog when she put her personal diary online in 1995.) Her latest site is described as "a metablog about Askspace's principles: wisdom of crowds, transparency, business ownership, Web 2.0."

A WORD FROM WE

"Wikipedia [has] bureaucrats, stewards, and administrators. These roles are formed either by election or promotion, and they possess blanket edit, deletion, or account revocation rights. The point to be made here is that intrinsic within the nature of self-governance of the Wikipedia is the presence of roles for monitoring and control, albeit democratic."

—CHANDRIKA SAMARTH, MEMBER OF THE WE ARE SMARTER COMMUNITY

In the first chapter of this book, we briefly discussed another effort to use crowdsourcing to perform a variety of roles, including that of management. Cambrian House relies on a community of 30,000 individuals to come up with new ideas, try them out, suggest improvements, and then connect with other interested members to build and commercialize it. Points toward a share of any eventual profit and cash up front are awarded to idea inventors and those who spend time adding or improving features. As of spring 2007, all four of the company's underwritten crowdsourced products were proceeding on course, with more than 200 other ideas under development by the Cambrian House community without any interference from the company itself.

cembrianhouse
home of crowdsourcing

So here we have a successful example of a community taking on some managerial duties, although there needs to be an asterisk beside that sentence. In the TBE project, the attempt was made to enlist the community in actually developing a chosen product—an attempt that eventually failed. At Cambrian, employees perform and manage some tasks (designing, manufacturing, and the like) if the company invests in or works directly with a community member's project.

Suffice it to say, then, that our two examples at least leave the door open to the possibility that communities will eventually be able to handle substantial management tasks. We're on much firmer ground, though, with the other business functions that the "power of we" taps.

08

Lead from the Rear

All through history, leaders have sought to persuade or compel communities to change their ways. The more drastic the change desired, the less likely the success. The "Great Leap Forward" of China's Communist leader Mao Zdong, for example, imposed a whole new political structure on his people in his rush to industrialize. It was a major disaster: Millions died of starvation, and the economy was devastated. Fifty years later, Mao's folly remains a cautionary tale for anyone who hopes to control the attitudes and actions of a group of independent people.

As we have argued throughout this book, wikinomic communities can often perform real-world tasks faster,

better, and cheaper than individuals. Bt building a successful community is no simple matter. Here, as in all aspects of business, from hiring to marketing, the price of great rewards is great risk. And that has never been so true as in the era of Web 2.0, when a seemingly minor mistake can snowball into a fatal disaster with lightning speed.

"I must follow the people. Am I not their leader?"

—BENJAMIN DISRAELI, BRITISH STATESMAN

This chapter lays out a series of guidelines intended to help
companies avoid some of the pitfalls along the 2.0 road.
They reflect the experience of leaders who have followed that
crowdsourcing route—men and women who have shared
their trials and triumphs on www.wearesmarter.org, the
online community we established on the way to writing
this book.

I. Lead from the Rear

It takes a company a lot of time, money, and effort to build
a community. Inevitably, the temptation arises to run it like
any other part of the enterprise. That's a bad idea. The whole
point of crowdsourcing is to
access the fresh, powerful ideas
and instincts of the community.
The company's role is to provide
direction and then stand back:
Interference with communal
processes defeats the purpose.

In other words, the company is not the star of the show, but
the producer, working from behind the scenes to make it

easy and comfortable for all community
members to get involved and stay
involved. The words and ideas should be
allowed to flow unimpeded:a collective
stream of consciousness. When
overzealous managers interrupt and
derail the conversation, valuable ideas
are lost.

As we mentioned at the start of the book, when Jeff Bezos opened Amazon's database to savvy outsiders, he didn't tell them what to do with it. He announced, "We're going to aggressively expose ourselves." He left it to the crowd to figure out how best to use the site, and he profited mightily.

2. Know When to Step In

Communities have built-in self-correcting capacities. Troublemakers get squelched or ignored;bad information gets corrected. On craigslist.org, for instance, whenever an ad breaks the site's terms of service—say, a seemingly personal appeal turns out to be a link to a Web site—or if a post is miscategorized or is really spam, the community members are all over it like a terrier chasing a cat. More than 25 percent of craigslist postings are flagged for removal by members, and of that number, an amazing 95 percent turn out to be violations.

Still, the threats to community operations are endless and often ingenious. Sometimes they come from those who have a special agenda in mind for the group—an outside marketer, say, who's hoping to capitalize on a group's size to peddle his or her own company's products or even hijack the community

to do his or her selling. Sometimes the threats are simply the work of twisted minds—so-called flamers, for example, who seek to entertain themselves by creating trouble. They like to post a controversial, hostile message on a community's site for the sole purpose of stirring up an angry response and a disruptive debate. Or the troublemaker could be a hacker, like the one we talked about in Chapter 3 "How May We Help We?", who wreaked havoc in Chapter 3"How May We Help We?", who wreaked havoc with PMI Audio's community forums.

When flamers or other intruders hinder a community's operations and remain unchecked, the company should not hesitate to step in. By the same token, if the misinformation being bandied about might cause someone to make a potentially harmful or costly mistake, managers owe it to the community—and to the company—to clarify ASAP. In all cases, though, such intrusions should be brief and hedged with explanations.

That same caveat applies to those moments when the community seems a tad too messy or even drifting toward chaos. Let's face it, people want to type in their own favorite

fonts, punctuate any way that suits them, and express themselves in idiosyncratic ways. Just like the folks who man the Cookshack forums back in Chapter 3they also will tell off-color stories, brag about their grandchildren, and generally wander off-topic. All this is understandable and even beneficial in principle:Original ideas often emerge from such spontaneous, off-the-cuff behavior. Communities thrive on the unexpected and the spontaneous.

Bt if communities wander too far from their mission for too long, company managers need to find ways to weigh in— summarizing the discussion, for example, to move it forward.

It can be tricky to maintain an unfettered environment that encourages original thinking yet never gets so tumultuous or off-point that it fails to function properly. Best to err on the side of *laissez-faire*. Otherwise, you'll never know how many groundbreaking concepts and comments your community was deprived of hearing.

And if you're relying on community members to perform a service function, consider following the path of companies such as ChaCha.com and eBay that ask customers to rate the service help they've been given.

3. Form a Club, a Real Community of Like-Minded People

Creating a vibrant community is all about creating a critical mass of good minds and spurring them to spark off each other. But the odds of success improve when the members share the same general outlook—it simply makes it easier for them to communicate and cooperate. Their energy is spent on the company's mission, not on quarreling over their differences. A mix of jocks and nerds, say, or left-wingers and right-wingers, is less likely to achieve the trust and commitment needed to evoke and maximize the group's collective knowledge. That thought must have weighed heavily with Virgin Mobile USA managers when they sifted through their list of online customers to create their 2,000-member "insiders" community, the one we talked about in Chapter 2, "Go from Me to We."

A company's first target group in forming a community should be those who have a clear interest in connecting with

the organization—satisfied customers, for example, or residents of towns where the company operates. The secondary goal is to enroll as many bright people

CREATING A VIBRANT COMMUNITY IS ALL ABOUT CREATING A CRITICAL MASS OF GOOD MINDS AND SPURRING THEM TO SPARK OFF EACH OTHER.

as possible. An exciting circle of like-minded people can be a magnet for others at a time when business needs all the good minds it can find.

Success today depends on amassing intellectual property, strengthening brands, and holding on to fickle customers, all of which require very smart people. They're in short supply, partly because of the newly global talent hunt and partly because talented people can pick and choose where they settle and dictate their own terms.

The bright people needed to create a vibrant community are likely to be so involved in the conversation that they carry it on beyond the virtual venue. Encourage them to do so, to keep talking and thinking about the community wherever they are. Suggest that they work the room at conferences and exchange phone calls, e-mail, and snail mail—anything to help members uncover shared interests, strengthen connections, and deepen personal bonds. Remember those offline meetings sponsored by the VirtualTourist community? The object of all such activities: a cohesive community that grows ideas with all the bursting vitality of a cornfield in July.

Size matters, too. The community must be large and smart enough to ride herd on the content it produces, catching and correcting mistakes and improper additions as they occur.

Generally, the bigger the collective brain, the greater the variety of viewpoints and information, and the better the content. As the members interact, they absorb one another's interests and expand their horizons so that what might have begun as a community focused on marketing, for instance, gradually branches out to innovate in other processes vital to its corporate sponsor.

4. You Can't Hide, So Don't Even Try

It's an inescapable truth of this transparent age that sooner or later—and, mostly, sooner—the errors a company commits will be exposed for everyone to see. When a mistake is made in working with a community, the best course is to admit it without delay, apologize, and make sure it's not repeated.

When an error surfaces, there's a natural inclination to hunker down and hope it will all go away. Companies put off responding—or, worse yet, erase e-mails and otherwise try to deny or pretend that nothing happened. Not a good idea. As we've seen "on the highest levels," cover-ups have a way of making matters worse.

The same goes for the tired old art of spinning, the biased and deceptive effort to put the best face on an unfavorable incident. Spin destroys the implied covenant a company has with its community and can create all sorts of havoc.

Take a lesson from CBS News. In spring 2007, in one of her "Notebook" segments on the company Web site, Katie Couric presented a piece that began "I still remember when I first got my library card." The problem, as the network learned too late, was that the rest of the piece had actually been written by a CB producer—and the producer, in turn, had actually stolen large chunks of it from an article in *The Wall Street Journal*. CB quickly went public with the story, replacing the piece with a "correction" and firing the offending producer. The network also explained that the ghostwriting of anchors' commentary was a routine practice ("That's the way television generally works," a spokeswoman said. "It's a very collaborative medium.")and that Couric did write some of her pieces.

There was a predictable uproar that took some time to settle down, partly because of Couric's high-profile, big-money debut as the first female evening-news anchor and her subsequent poor showing in the ratings. Bt CB was able to contain the damage by its decision to go public with the error and its willingness to explain the process used to prepare the "Notebook" segments.

The bottom line is this:In a world where the inner workings of government and business are daily revealed through e-mails, companies need to erase the word *confidential* from their mental hard drives. The whistleblowers reign supreme, abetted by those ever-more-powerful online search engines whose algorithms don't distinguish between good news and bad.

So if a company's reputation with its community is tarnished by some misstep, denials and evasions are the wrong way to go. The company needs to 'fess up, explain how it happened, and transgress no more. P.S. It might also find some creative ways to let the community know about the positive things the company has accomplished lately.)

5. Forget about Perfection

Anything that gets members of a
community talking is good. Anything that
slows that conversation is bad. When a
company communication is too flashy or
too finely tuned, it can rapidly shut down
discussion and make it impossible to get the
valuable feedback the company seeks.

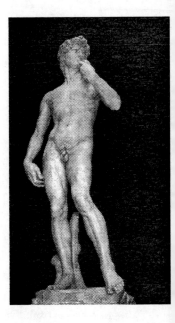

We all experience the phenomenon in our
daily lives. We're sitting with friends or
family around the kitchen table or at the
neighborhood bar, the banter and easy talk
bouncing back and forth, when
a newcomer joins in. There's
nothing really wrong with
him—he's pleasant and articulate, offering
very intelligent, cogent opinions and ideas—
but somehow his presence is an intrusion. The
jokes fall flat. The flights of fancy are grounded.

That's more or less what happens when companies' messages
are too perfect, too polished. Overly explained and edited
topical material makes people feel as if everything has already
been said, thus deterring them from jumping in with their
own observations and opinions. Instead, many companies
adopt a comfortable, down-home tone, and some even
sprinkle their remarks with grammatical or spelling errors.
The object is to give the company a human face and avoid
language that might be seen as officious or patronizing.

Southwest Airlines, long admired as the master of the
discounters, is also a master at communicating with its
communities. Its "Nts About Southwest" blog, for example,

is written by different employees each month but is open to customers and the public as well. They weigh in with comments and complaints. That's why the company likens the blog to an "online watercooler." The blogs and the comments are all part of a comfortable, easygoing conversation that ensures the company of an interested, involved community of employees and customers.

Just how involved was made clear in 2006 when a blog by CEO Gary Kelly reported that the company might change its, if you will, long-standing open-seating policy. Hundreds of customers and employees complained at the prospect of being told where to sit. As they made clear, Southwest's unique first-come seating policy had been one reason customers kept coming back. Open seating was saved. By starting an unscripted conversation with customers, Southwest got some invaluable firsthand feedback from the people who foot its bills and pay its employees' salaries.

The tidy perfection of polished presentations is the wrong tack to take with a community.

6. Stir Things Up

There's nothing quite so blah and unproductive as a homogeneous, complacent community Web site. The sponsoring company is looking for new ideas, instructive feedback, and a glimpse of future customer trends. Instead, it sees nothing but platitudes and familiar comments—many of them favorable, to be sure, but none of them truly helpful. It's time for the company to step in and stir things up.

What's needed is a real debating club, one in which all viewpoints on a particular topic are welcome. Companies need to make sure that contrary opinions are encouraged, that members start challenging the revealed wisdoms of the group. It's in the play of argument and counterargument that fresh ideas rise to the surface.

Glenn Kelman, CEO of the online real estate brokerage firm Redfin, embraced contrariness with a passion when he decided to "tell all" online and allow his competitors to savage him in plain sight of customers.

As recounted by Clive Thompson in the April 2007 issue of *Wired* magazine, Kelman raised the hackles of old-line real estate agents when he sliced commissions for sellers to about a third of the typical rate. His rivals retaliated by refusing to sell houses to anyone who used Redfin's service.

Kelman suffered in silence for months. Then he took to blogging. But he also shined the hot light of publicity on his competitors' greedy practices, while allowing them to freely state their cases via comments on the company's Web site. They let fly with nasty comments, and Kelman returned fire with his own zingers.

Potential homebuyers loved tuning in for the next episode in the battle of the brokers, and that began to make Kelman's

enemies nervous. They realized that airing their industry's dirty laundry in public might not be good for anyone's business, but they were only partially right.

Redfin's revenues were growing. By presenting both sides of the debate and being honest about his own mistakes and problems, he had created an online community of sympathetic would-be customers.

The goal is to create a site that touches people where they live, that elicits involvement and passion—and that means finding the right proposition. One example we pointed to was Zebo. com, whose success is based on the fact that young people are passionate about what they own and want to own.

7. Say Thank You

Companies that sponsor communities need to remember that a transaction is taking place. The members of the communities are sharing themselves and their talents in ways that have value for the companies, and their contributions deserve to be acknowledged and rewarded.

Gather.com, for instance, uses a point system to reward member participation. The more its members join in the discussion, the more points they earn for spending on goods and services provided by Gather's partners. People who frequently contribute quality content to the site can even earn cash rewards.

As indicated in earlier chapters, different companies take different approaches. Some, such as P&G, keep active community members in the loop with news about upcoming products and samples of the same. Others, such as InnoCentive, hold out the possibility of making thousands of dollars if a community member can solve a scientific problem. Whatever approach a company plans to take to thank its community, the community should first review it to make sure it is perceived as fair and adequate. Anything less will defeat the purpose and leave the members frustrated and annoyed.

Many communities, such as Gather.com, reward their top contributors, but not everyone has equal access to a computer, and many people have a lifestyle that permits only infrequent contributions. Moreover, one provocative or brilliant post can outweigh a string of mundane comments. It's important for companies to remember those members whose value is very real but cannot be easily measured by number of contributions.

8. This Is Not a One-Night Stand

Communities take time to develop. Attracting a cast of valuable characters who share common interests cannot be accomplished overnight, and establishing and strengthening the personal relationships so necessary to a productive environment is a long-term proposition. This should not be rushed. You might remember our description of Current TV, the station Al Gore helped create, which critics wrote off after a slow start;it's doing just fine now, thank you very much.

While the community is forming, companies need to experiment with content and ways of inciting valuable discussion. Community members themselves should be enlisted in that process, providing feedback and their own suggestions for keeping the idea pot bubbling. At the same

time, companies would do well to help members improve
their collaborative abilities, perhaps by encouraging them to
get involved in other collaborative environments.

Above all, sponsors should pay attention, observing the
interactions and flow of ideas within their communities and
monitoring community reactions to the sponsors' initiatives.
Sponsors need to develop their own sets of goals for their
communities and to establish target dates for the
evaluation of their virtual ventures. For a new
group, a year or 18 months is soon enough to
make a determination of whether the game has
been worth the candle.

At the start of this book, we described the revolutionary
impact that communities are having on the way business is
conducted—their ability to devise new products and services,
provide customer service, improve sales and manufacturing,
and tap into new sources of financing. We also promised to
help you better understand how to make that happen in your
own company by organizing, inspiring, and maintaining your
own community. As we reach the end of our journey together,
we sincerely hope that we have lived up to that promise.

But whatever your feelings are
about this book, we urge you to
continue your exploration of the
crowdsourcing phenomenon.
It is the wave of the future, and
you should be riding it.

Speaking of the future, in the pages just ahead, we offer a
short afterword about the tremendous transformation that is
taking place in the nature of work, including the relationship
between companies and their employees. You'll not be
surprised, we suspect, to find that we—and large numbers
of experts—believe that communities of workers will have a
starring role.

Afterword—Join the Crowd

In his 1990 hit play *Six Degrees of Separation*, John Guare has one of his characters say, "I read somewhere that everybody on this planet is separated by only six other people.  ... The President of the United States, a gondolier in Venice, just fill in the names. I find it extremely comforting that we're so close."

That six-degree equation evolved from the 1967 experiment of a social psychologist named Stanley Milgram, who had volunteers mail packages to 100 people at random. Columbia University professors repeated the experiment in 2002, but this time it was via e-mail, and some 60,000 people from 166 nations participated. The result, though, was pretty much the same. An average of no more than six links separated one e-mailer from another. Whether you find that comforting, though, is another matter.

 The world as we've known it is changing all around us, and a big part of that change is in the nature of the connections between people and between people

and their employers. Computers, cell phones, iPods, and the Internet are making us more distinctly individual and independent. We spend more time away from the office, working and traveling, and a great deal more time online, accessing information for our work and communicating with colleagues, suppliers, and customers. Although the Internet has made workers more independent, it has also led them to create communities built upon collaboration. In other words, our degree of separation from our customary work life has increased, while, at the same time, we have never been so widely connected.

Experts such as Gartner Inc., a Connecticut-based technology research and advisory company, expect that these developments will drastically alter the nature of work over the next decade. Freed from dependence upon the company for infrastructure and resources, employees will provide intangible services from their own personally customized workspaces. They will rely on networks of people, many of them unaffiliated with their employer, for advice, information, and best practices.

Inevitably, their relationship to the company will be transformed. The expertise they have chosen and developed will allow them to move easily from one employer to another, erasing whatever vestiges of company loyalty remain. They will insist that collaboration, much of it remote, replace the traditional authoritarian interactions of manager and employee. As Gartner put it in a recent report, the new relationship will be one of symbiosis. Indeed, we believe that the corporation as it now exists, with its armies of salaried workers in identical cubicles, will gradually disappear. Instead, there will be virtual communities that will be able to mobilize teams of specialists to take on necessary tasks for customers.

FREED FROM DEPENDENCE UPON THE COMPANY FOR
INFRASTRUCTURE AND RESOURCES, EMPLOYEES
WILL PROVIDE INTANGIBLE SERVICES FROM THEIR
OWN PERSONALLY CUSTOMIZED WORKSPACES.

How rapidly is the U.S. moving toward a virtual life? According to the Kaiser Family Foundation, between 1999 and 2004, children's time on the computer doubled, along with huge increases in their hours spent in chat rooms, interactive channels, and instant messaging. When they grow up, online connectedness will seem like the obvious option for play or work.

For now, though, the work changes we have discussed are still early days—companies have plenty of time to prepare to meet them. Leaders need to examine their management and support policies, and adjust them to fit the more collaborative model

their newly independent employees seek. A policy carved in stone simply doesn't suffice for the new-breed workers who thrive on challenge and are constantly seeking out-of-the-box assignments that will boost their expertise. At the same time, companies should become knowledgeable about the care and feeding of virtual networks and communities, which play such an important role in the work life of the newly independent worker.

One way to get started is to join us on our Web site, **www.wearesmarter.org**.

You might recall that we introduced the site back in the introduction to this book. We had hoped the members would actually write the book for us. That did not happen, but they have continued to offer their insights, sharing their experiences and best practices with other members.

We hope the readers of this book will join our community, not only to benefit from the posts of other members and from the occasional in-person meetings, but to share with us their own stories. That seems to us the best of all possible worlds, with business getting smarter by tapping the collective brainpower of community.

Company Index

Name Index

Subject Index

Acknowledgments

Since the premise of this project was to involve a large number of people in the creative process, writing a brief acknowledgements section is a unique challenge. But the contributions of a small group of people stand out and deserve to be highlighted.

Tim Moore, Vice President at Pearson and Publisher of both Prentice Hall and The Financial Times Press, provided discipline when we most needed it—best summed up by his typical refrain, "Hey, folks, we need to get this community up and running and a book from them finished."

Tim and the Pearson team were the project's emotional drivers relying equally on enthusiasm, irritation, and encouragement to keep us moving toward an actual, tangible end product from this groundbreaking social networking project. Tim's prodding and his willingness to view the process as an experiment helped immensely, and we are grateful for his and his team's encouragement and support.

Donna Carpenter and Maurice (Mo) Coyle drove the bulk of the research and the writing which was derived from the community's contributions and from leaders in the social networking market. They are masters of the written word, and their skills are largely what made the contributions of the community so readable and easy for those interested in social networking in their companies to understand. This is not the first book that has benefited from their unique abilities and, we are certain, it will not be their last in partnership with emerging business communities. We deeply appreciate their efforts.

Isaac Hazard had the most difficult job among us—to coordinate the day-to-day activities of the community and all of its constituents. To say he did so with grace and calm would be a gross understatement; a better characterization would be to note that despite the chaos and panic that engulfed a community-oriented project on a regular basis, Isaac kept everyone on track and, somehow, got the community to work as "one"—sharing their collective wisdom with each other. Thank you, Isaac.

Tom Malone from MIT was deeply involved in the design of many aspects of the community, from the approach to offer incentives to the community contributors to the open source license we used to capture the wisdom of the community. He brought an academic's discipline to the discussion, and reminded us that we were engaged not only to publish a book but to experiment with a process that was unique and groundbreaking. His questions and ideas significantly strengthened the initiative, for which we are grateful.

Jerry Wind from The Wharton School supported this community initiative from its earliest days, and we are proud to publish this book under Prentice Hall banner. Jerry has an extraordinary ability to see value in ideas from their earliest stage of conception, but also to add value to those ideas at every stage of development. His contributions are much appreciated especially during the most difficult moments.

Finally, we are indebted to a group of people we have never met, and who—as far as we know—have never met each other. Ten individuals from our community volunteered to be "chapter leaders" to help monitor and guide the discussion of various chapters in the book. They did so when the role of chapter leader was largely undefined, and they performed their role ably and without compensation or (until now) recognition: Lilly Evans, Ryan Mykita, Greg Krauska, Margot Sayers, Olivier Amprimo, Joe Flumerfelt, Rich Luker, Bruce Hazard, Mel Aclaro, and Rui Monteiroour deepest thanks. The project could not have proceeded without you.

We were also ably assisted by a tremendous team. Many thanks to:

Shared Insights

Michael Libert
Isaac Hazard
Charlotte Daher
Robin Rose
Joe Tremonte
Shanon Mckenna
Shannon Di Gregorio
Mia Encarnacion

Jim Storer
Gary Bellardino
Aaron Strout
Erika Halloran
Mark Wallace
Chris Edwards
Stephen Marcus

Marketing, PR, and Design

Peter Himler
Giles Dickerson

Mark Fortier

Pearson

Tim Moore
Pamela Boland
Julie Phifer
Megan Colvin
Kristy Hart
Jake McFarland

Amy Neidlinger
Russ Hall
Amy Fandrei
Gina Kanouse
Cheryl Lenser
Dan Uhrig

Wharton

Carol Orenstein
Tracy Simon

Yoram (Jerry) Wind
Matt Schuler

Wordworks

Donna Carpenter
Ruth Hlavacek
Cindy Butler Sammons

Maurice Coyle
Larry Martz
Robert W. Stock

MIT

Thomas Malone
Sean Brown
Tammy Cupples

Stephen Buckley
Paul Denning

Legal

Scott Soloway

Karen Rivard

Chapter Moderators

Lilly Evans
Greg Krauska
Olivier Amprimo
Rich Luker
Mel Aclaro

Ryan Mykita
Margot Sayers
Joe Flumerfelt
Bruce Hazard
Rui Monteiro

Board Advisors

Philip Evans

Jimmy Wales

The Helen Rees Literary Agency

Helen Rees

Joan Mazmanian